When Love Broke Through

FINDING FAITH, COURAGE, AND LOVE IN THE STORM

Nicole Body

FIRST EDITION

ISBN: 978-1-946466-83-9

Library of Congress Control Number: 2020922964

Published by

3741 Linden Avenue SE | Grand Rapids, MI 49548

Printed in the United States

To my husband, Wes

You are the greatest joy within my soul and the keeper of my heart. I love you with every ounce of my being. Thank you for the immeasurable ways you love me. Life with you has been the most beautiful dance. I am looking forward to the next dance number.

Table of Contents

Introduction

You know the saying "Love is blind."

Well, that's the way ours started.

Wes and I were set up on a blind date where we met at a coffee shop in a small town in Colorado. I was instantaneously captivated by his blue eyes and smile, and the conversation had been entrancing as well.

When he asked me to dinner after coffee, I was charmed and thought it might have been a good sign that the date was going well. I'm typically not a nervous person, but when I realized that I was genuinely interested in him I started acting awkward.

As we walked up to the restaurant, I blurted out a question that comes highly *not* recommended:

"So where do you see yourself in five years?" I asked.

I winced as I realized how cheesy that was for me to ask, having just met him.

That's it. I blew it. Take a good look into those beautiful eyes at dinner because that's certainly the last time you're going to see them.

He looked over at me and smiled as though he knew I had put my foot in my mouth. He shifted his gaze forward and kept walking for a few steps before sharing his answer with me.

"I don't know where I'll be or what I'll be doing," he said as I was thinking I had completely ruined my chances with him. "I hope that if I'm married to someone, our eyes are looking ahead in the same direction together in faith."

I can't believe I asked such an awkward question and received such a profound reply. I think I might be in love. I hope I still have a chance with him. This could be something special.

And just over a year later we got married.

He had swept me off my feet from the moment I met him, and I was bewildered that I could continue to grow in love with someone so much. In some ways, we were exactly the same and in other ways, we were perfect opposites.

Wes is charming, methodical, and kind. He has a calmness about him that brings people at ease when they are in his presence. His personality fits like a puzzle piece with my loud, spontaneous, and adventurous heart.

One thing that was equally important to us both, though, was our faith.

We both saw scripture in unique ways and learned from each other when we studied together. During our time reading with one another, I found a verse that framed the lens of my life. I memorized it and I referred to it as my "life verse."

> *I have told you these things, so that in me you may have peace. In this world, you will have trouble. But take heart! I have overcome the world.* (John 16:33, NIV)

It was through that verse and our relationship where I learned that true love is not blind at all.

It is intentional. It is a choice. It endures. It sees the truth and loves even then.

Love overcomes.

No wall can keep it out. No hardship can stop it. No voice can drown it.

Love breaks through.

Although we couldn't say exactly where we would be or what we would be doing in the years to come, we could remain anchored in what we knew through our faith:

We will have trouble. We can take heart. Jesus has overcome.

But I thought certainly it would be way down the road before I would truly need that verse—for the hard stuff at least. We were in our twenties and had our entire lives ahead of us. We were young, deeply in love, and ready to venture into the world together.

So I put that verse in my back pocket in case I needed it for a rainy day—as it is often said: "When it rains it pours."

I hoped it would serve as a sturdy umbrella when a storm arrived.

1

Hawaiian Dreams

Three, two, one . . . and we're off!

Our double tube launched down the mountain-sized water slide and began whipping around every turn. Views of the Hawaiian mountains and ocean disappeared as we picked up speed and water splashed in our eyes at our resort's waterpark. Our laughter was roaring in intervals as it was repeatedly drowned out by the water that crashed into our faces. It had been the perfect way to spend our last day of vacation on the beautiful island of Oahu at the Disney Aulani Resort and Spa as we celebrated our three-year wedding anniversary.

"Do you remember the words I said to you in my vows?" Wes asked me with a grin on his face quickly getting out of the water. We were still laughing from the experience when he stretched out his hand to help me out of the pool.

"Only like you spoke them to me yesterday," I replied as smitten as could be while he pulled me up on the side of the pool. I awaited what romantic words he would say as I was now wrapped up in his arms.

"I'm glad you remember," he replied nodding curiously while he suspiciously looked around. "Then you know that I never promised that I wouldn't do this!"

He leaned down swiftly, placed his arms in the crease of my legs, scooped me up, and launched us both back into the water. The splash sent water up my nose and my long, wet hair was tangled all over my face.

"Oh, you sure think you're funny, don't you?" I asked him while coming up for air and laughing while I dunked him. He jumped up and smiled back at me.

"I can't believe we're leaving today," I said while we swam toward the shallow end of the water. "It's been the most perfect week away together. Thank you for taking me here to celebrate."

"Well, almost perfect," he said.

"What do you me—" I started to ask before finding myself underwater being dunked.

"*Now* we can say it's been the perfect week," he said as I floated in his arms while shaking my head, chuckling.

"They say marriage is all about balance," I said, laughing. "I guess now we're even with dunks."

He had made me smile every day since I met him and somehow uncovered new ways to make my heart swoon even after three years of marriage.

This vacation had been just what my heart needed. We couldn't complain about going home, though, because we resided in the beautiful state of Colorado with an unrestricted view of the Rocky Mountains out our back window.

We did know that going back home was going to be emotional. My parents had just announced that they would be moving from Colorado to Houston in a couple of weeks for my dad's job. Even though I grew up in Texas, I didn't see Wes and I moving there.

My dad had a gift for making people laugh. There was no way you could be in his presence for very long without him saying something to make you crack a smile. I had only ever seen him cry twice and knew that was too many times in his mind. He liked keeping the mood light and he was good at it. It was fitting that my mom was married to him since she had the best laugh of anyone I knew.

This move would put a thousand miles between us. I was close with my family and loved spending time with them and their two golden retrievers. It had been wonderful living close by one another, but now I was realizing that this season was coming to an end and it was hard.

"Smile for me," Wes requested with his face exaggerated with joy. He must have noticed I was lost in thought.

I obliged as I awkwardly showed him all my teeth without forming a traditional smile.

"That's my girl," he said tucking my hair behind my ear, laughing. "You're beautiful—do you know that?"

I believed he meant the words he said. The problem was that *I* didn't believe it.

I had gained quite a bit of weight over the last couple of years and I didn't feel beautiful in the slightest. Shortly after we got married I had developed what seemed like an intolerance to food altogether. Every time I had eaten over the last three years I would get sick. I had gone through extensive testing ordered by different doctors, but no one could figure out what was wrong.

Depression had sunk in with the many failed attempts to find a cure to this ailment, so my relationship with food had gotten bad. I ate anything I wanted to without restraint since I knew I would be in pain no matter what.

Somehow, though, he still thought I was pretty, and it gave me hope that maybe one day I could love myself the way he loved me. I was just thankful that I didn't feel sick while we wrapped up the last day of our trip.

"How about one more go at the slide?" Wes suggested as he jumped back out of the water.

"That sounds great," I said, getting out to help carry the double tube up for one more time down the slide.

"Baby, I love you," he said tenderly.

"I love you too."

I shook my head in disbelief that this kind of love existed. He was full of joy and life and knew just what to say and do to light a fire within my soul.

Wes motioned his hand at me to follow him as he had purposely allowed us to fall behind so we could run up the stairs. When we reached the top, we both got situated on the tube.

"Let's make this ride the best one yet," I said, turning around right before we launched down the slide together.

"Here's to the end of our anniversary trip in Hawaii," Wes shouted as he pushed our tube down the slide.

It traveled like a rocket as we leaned hard on each turn to go as high up on the sides of the slide as we could. The water rushed over us as we almost toppled the tube from the height and speed that we were reaching with every twist.

When our tube roared across the water at the end of the slide, it whipped aggressively toward the left unlike it had before. We noticed that we were approaching a wall quickly and the only thing that would stop the crash was my foot.

Crack.

My foot slammed into the wall, making a loud noise. We slowly spun around and eventually, our inner tube stopped.

"Are you okay?" Wes shouted from behind me.

"I've never been better!" I replied, filled with adrenaline while Wes cheered in the back. "We survived!"

"That was the perfect way to end our trip!" he exclaimed as we got off the tube to head back inside our resort room to change.

We gathered all our belongings and drove to the airport to head back home. When we boarded the plane, Wes leaned over to me to kiss me on the cheek.

"What a great week!" he said with a tired smile.

"It sure was," I replied, noticing pain developing in my foot. "I couldn't have asked for anything more wonderful. Except I might need to see a doctor about my foot when we get back. This might be a problem."

"Oh, no," he said as we both made our way to our seats on the airplane and sat down. "From the slide? We'll schedule you an appointment as soon as we get back."

"You should get some rest," I suggested noticing Wes' eyes were almost completely shut already.

"Okay," he replied with eyes now closed. "I'll see you in a little while."

I tried for hours to fall asleep but my foot started throbbing and my mind wouldn't stop racing. I decided to take my phone out to look at some of the pictures we took to pass the time on the flight.

I was captivated by the waterfalls, the ocean, and the mountains in the background from the ATV excursion we had taken. Each photo was full of beauty, fun, and excitement.

Nothing had been more enchanting to me than the hike we went on at Manoa Falls. It was gigantic and lush and I felt so alive there. It was the closest visual in my mind of how the Garden of Eden looked when no blemish had yet entered into the world. The thick greenery continued as far as the eye could see. There were many kinds of vegetation unified together that created the most stunning place I had ever seen.

"I love that picture." I heard Wes say causing me to jump in my seat. I was startled that he was awake and looking over my shoulder. "The way the sunlight hits your hair in this photo—you're absolutely stunning."

I laughed as he knew how hard it was for me to receive compliments from him like that.

"I believe you'll see what I see one day," he said confidently and compassionately. “Your beauty, your worth, God’s handiwork. You are so loved.”

He squeezed my hand and it was like a boost of energy.

“Can you believe I cried as we were leaving Manoa Falls?” I asked, redirecting his attention to the photo.

“How could I forget?” he asked rhetorically. “You were mesmerized. It was like you saw heaven.”

“It was a perfect moment for me: standing next to the love of my life in the most beautiful place I had ever seen,” I explained. “However, as wonderful as it was, I’m excited to be heading back home.”

The flight attendants started making their way down the aisles to collect trash, so we knew we were getting close to Colorado.

“That’s neat, babe.” He turned more toward me to listen intentionally. “What are you most looking forward to?”

“I’m looking forward to spending time with my parents before they move,” I shared. “And honestly, I just love doing life with you. I can’t wait to see what adventures are up ahead!”

“We’re preparing the cabin for our descent into Denver,” the flight attendant said over the intercom. “Fasten your seatbelts. It is going to be a turbulent descent.”

We buckled our seatbelts and prepared for the turbulence that lay ahead.

2

Highs and Lows

Although we missed Hawaii, it felt nice to be settled back at home and sleeping in our own bed. Our house was an older, split-level layout with light brown carpeted stairs that crunched when you stepped on them. We loved every quirk and crack it displayed. It was our first house together and it encapsulated the best years of my life up to that point.

Two weeks had passed since my parents moved to Houston and we found ourselves in the middle of June. We missed them and knew that they were missing the cool Colorado summer since Houston was hot during that time of year.

Each weekend during the summer Wes and I would always seek activities outdoors so we could enjoy the beautiful weather together. On that particular weekend, we hadn't made any plans yet.

"I have an exciting idea," Wes said to me in the kitchen.

"Oh, tell me, tell me!" I replied with anticipation. "What's on your mind?"

"My uncle is in town and I thought we could host my family for a barbecue tonight."

"I love that idea," I said as I moved closer to him in the kitchen. "I have a few requests for consideration, if I may."

"Let's see if I can oblige," he said while wrapping his arms around my waist, flirting with me.

"First I'm going to need lots of rhinestones."

"What?" he asked, laughing. "What do rhinestones have to do with a barbecue?"

"Well, since I'm in an orthopedic boot now from fracturing my foot on the slide in Hawaii, I would like to bedazzle the boot before your family arrives," I explained, giggling. "I shared the idea with my doctor and he said it was a fabulous idea."

It turned out that I indeed needed a large black orthopedic boot to house my foot since I injured it on our vacation. I had a new doctor and he advised that I should wear it as long as I was experiencing discomfort, which he said would be anywhere from one to two months.

"I agree with your doctor that it's an excellent idea," he said as he kissed his hand and reached down to my boot as if to transfer it there. "I'm glad we found you a doctor who appreciates your sparkly spirit! What else do we need for our barbecue?"

"Chicken, hamburgers, and jalapeño poppers," I said, thinking of all the delicious things that make a barbecue great. "And one more very important thing."

"What's that?"

"I would like giant marshmallows," I said, stretching my hands out wide. "The largest ones we can find. It's not an official barbecue without s'mores."

"I couldn't agree more. Let's call my family, head to the store, and get ready for a great night!"

Wes' parents and extended family began arriving as the sun slowly started falling behind the mountain range. My mother-in-law and father-in-law greeted us with big hugs. They always had the best stories to share, so I was looking forward to time around the firepit.

"Look at your sparkly boot!" my mother-in-law exclaimed. "It's adorable—but I'm sorry you have to wear it."

"Thank you, Kathy," I replied, laughing while pouring her a glass of lemonade.

Kathy always made me smile. She was jubilant and joyous. She could turn every situation into a positive and even made wearing an orthopedic boot feel like an exciting adventure for me. She and my father-in-law, Bode, had been together for over forty years and were still completely in love. Bode was jovial and kind. He had embraced me as if I were his own daughter. Being surrounded by them was just what my heart needed while I was missing my family in Texas.

As the night commenced, Wes' uncle strummed his guitar and filled the backyard with beautiful music that floated on the crisp Colorado air to make for a next-to-perfect night. Wes grasped my waist so he could dance with me while the music was playing.

"This isn't going to be as easy as usual with me having this boot on and all," I said.

"I think we can manage," he said with a wink and slowly spun me. "Plus, we can be tonight's entertainment."

"You're too funny," I replied, engaging in his playful banter. "We should probably ask the crowd's definition of 'entertainment' first."

Dancing had been a precious part of our relationship since we had met, and it didn't surprise me at all that during a special night like this he would find a way for us to dance with one another. I was wobbly but it was lovely in every way as I pressed my cheek into his collarbone and rested my head while we swayed to the rhythm of the guitar.

After his uncle finished the song, I could hear Kathy from across the backyard telling her favorite story of her with Bode from many years ago. I walked over and caught the ending of it.

"And then I hit the mattress with my hand," she said, barely able to hold back her laughter. "And the spider flew straight up into the air and landed right back in the same spot. We screamed!"

Every person roared with laughter while they finished roasting marshmallows for s'mores.

I stood near the crackling fire and smiled at Kathy and Bode. They were sitting close together and laughing hysterically while reflecting on that moment together. She had her hand on his knee and their eyes gleamed while they looked at each other. I felt grateful for this family I had been blessed to join by marriage.

When we couldn't eat another bite of food and everyone was ready to head home, we said our goodbyes and then spent the next hour cleaning up. Wes and I recalled the stories told from the evening and chuckled even more together.

"Thank you for tonight, Wes," I said to him. "You are a wonderful husband."

We headed upstairs and got ready for bed. After finishing my nightly routine, I sat in bed next to him, started pulling the covers over me, and lay down.

"Oh, my!" I exclaimed as I threw the covers off me and sat up quickly.

"What's wrong, honey?" Wes asked, sitting up beside me.

"I think I'm going to be sick," I said as I placed my hands over my mouth.

I stood up anticipating the sickness to subside, but it didn't. Wes worriedly watched my every move as I limped back and forth at the end of the bed.

"Are you okay?" he asked, extremely concerned. "Let me help you get your boot back on so you don't hurt your foot more than it already is."

"I'll be okay," I said completely out of breath. "I just need a few minutes and it should go away."

I leaned over the edge of the bed and took a few deep breaths.

"I guess I had too much barbecue." I tried to make light of it as I didn't want to be dramatic. "Texas-sized marshmallows must have gotten the best of me!"

After twenty minutes of pacing and deep breathing, I felt that I might be able to lie down again. I slowly pushed the covers back and eased my body into bed as if to test the waters. As soon as I was lower than a seated posture, the feeling of pain from my stomach made its way back up to my throat.

"Oh, no," I said with wide eyes while sweat surfaced over my entire body.

I jumped out of bed as quickly as I could, gripping my stomach. The stomach problems and reflux had been going on for years, but nothing had happened quite like this before.

"Ouch, ouch, ouch!" I exclaimed with each step I took as I swiftly hobbled to the bathroom with no time to put my boot on. My knees hit the floor as my clammy hands gripped the sides of the toilet.

What is going on with me?

Fifteen minutes had felt like forever. I was out of breath and shaking.

"Do we need to go to the emergency room?" Wes asked quietly as he knelt down next to me while he gently rubbed my lower back.

"No, no, honey," I said, slowly pushing myself up from my knees. "I don't think I can lie down, though. I may have to sleep sitting up tonight."

"Okay," he said as he scooped me up off the cold laminate on the bathroom floor. I was trying to hold back tears as he set me down onto the edge of the bed. "Let me put your boot back on just in case, and we can put on a movie until you're able to fall asleep."

"I think I may have to stand up because even sitting down is making me nauseated now."

Wes wrapped a blanket around me and stood behind me with his arms around my shoulders. We swayed back and forth. Tears slowly rolled down my cheeks one by one until they reached my chin and splashed onto his forearm. My soft sobs were met with tender squeezes to let me know he wasn't going anywhere.

The pain slowly began to subside. When I couldn't stand another moment, he began arranging pillows that would surround me and placed some against the headboard of our bed to help me get situated. When I looked toward the headboard, I noticed the decoration that hung above it. It was a dark-colored panel with white cursive words painted on it: *I have found the one whom my soul loves.*

I hadn't looked at it in a while, but I was glad I caught sight of it that night.

I arranged the pillows around me while sitting up and finally got into a position that was comfortable enough to fall asleep.

"We'll call your new doctor on Monday if you aren't feeling better," Wes said, squeezing my hand. "Maybe he'll be different from prior doctors you've seen and can find a solution for your pain."

"I hope so," I said while fading into sleep. "I'm grateful I have you beside me tonight."

"I wouldn't be anywhere else."

In a complete state of exhaustion, I fell asleep.

3

Unexpected

The weekend ended and I still felt horrible. I let my supervisor, Lisa, at work know that I couldn't make it into work that day and called my doctor's office to see if I could come in for an emergency visit. Unfortunately, they informed me that my provider wasn't available that day.

"Is there anyone there I *can* see?" I begged over the phone.

"We can schedule you an appointment with his colleague, Dr. Odekirk if that works for you," the receptionist said.

"Yes, thank you," I said. "I can come in anytime."

Dr. Odekirk was an older gentleman. I learned that he worked only one and a half days each week as he was transitioning into retirement. He was kind, professional, and a great listener as I shared what brought me there that day.

During an abdominal assessment, I felt a searing pain near my gallbladder, so he ordered some tests for it to be checked. My gallbladder had been tested a handful of times in the last couple of years, but it always came back clear. I didn't have any expectation that they would find something, but I felt terrible and was willing to do anything.

When the date arrived for my CT scan, I learned I would need an IV in my arm. This was new from previous CT scans that I had undergone so it took me by surprise. Needles and I don't have the best history, since I typically pass out during a routine flu shot. I kept reminding myself that it would be over soon.

I can do this.

When I was finally taken back to be connected to the IV line, I met the CT technician who would assist with the appointment.

"The sensation that the IV contrast will give you will make you feel like you wet your pants," she told me. "Your hands and mouth may feel tingly, too, but the sensation will go away."

I nodded my head, humored by this news, and adjusted the pep talk to myself.

I can do this, but now I might wet my pants. Okay, I did not see my day going this way.

I lay down on the long, thin track that led to the donut-shaped opening where the machine would scan my body. The entire room was white and gray and left me feeling chilled. I had my arms stretched out behind my head so the IV contrast could be administered properly when it was time to do so.

"Hold your breath," the electronic voice from the machine instructed while maneuvering my extended body slowly in and out. "Now breathe."

It was normal enough. I had done this many times before.

"I'm going to administer the contrast now," I heard the CT tech say, her voice muffled over the sound system.

Oh, this is new.

The contrast flowed in like a rushing wave and I felt pressure in my arm. Suddenly my face and body felt hot and sweaty. Without missing a beat, the tingling feeling covered me.

Yep. I am fairly certain I just wet my pants.

"Hold your breath," the scanner instructed me once more. "Now breathe."

The tingling slowly started to go away but I couldn't tell quite yet if my pants were dry or not since my hands were still stretched behind my head.

My eyes widened as she began walking toward me.

I locked my widened eyes with hers as she walked toward me. She smiled as though she knew exactly what I was thinking.

"You didn't wet your pants," she said, chuckling as she took my IV out. "You did great."

"I am very glad that's over," I said after I made a quick check and laughed along with her. "I hope I never have to do *that* again!"

"Go enjoy the rest of your day and drink plenty of water," she said as she waved goodbye.

There was nothing like a little comic relief to help with continued pain. I smiled all the way to the car and couldn't wait to tell Wes.

I looked at the time and saw it was just after 3:00 p.m. I was unsure of whether or not I should head to work, so I called Lisa to check-in.

I told her about the CT scan and we laughed together. She was not only a talented and hardworking boss, but she had also become a trusted friend in my life.

"It's already after three," she said over the phone. "Go ahead and take the rest of the day off since the workday is nearly over anyway. Take care of yourself and let me know how you're feeling tomorrow."

After we got off the phone, I called to update Wes. I was completely exhausted and was ready to get back home.

I began wondering when I would receive the results. In my prior experience, tests could take a week or more before I would hear anything, but I was hoping that it would be sooner so I could find relief.

When I arrived home, Wes was still at work. It took me a couple of hours to find a way to comfortably position myself on the couch that would balance nausea and pain, but I eventually got settled. I was fully focused on not moving.

Buzz. Buzz.

My phone was ringing, and it was out of my arms' reach.

Oh, man—do I need to get this? I finally got situated. Maybe it's Wes. I should get it.

I shifted my body across the couch to pick up the phone. It was a number I didn't recognize.

"Hello," I said as I placed my legs on the floor and used my arms to push up to a seated position.

"Hi, Nicole," the voice on the line said. "This is Dr. Odekirk."

"Oh, hi," I said with surprise. My scan had been taken only a couple of hours ago and it wasn't typical to hear from a doctor this quickly. "How are you doing?"

The pain intensified. I slowly tried to recreate my original positioning on the couch to relieve the pain so I could have a conversation with him.

"I'm doing well," he said. "Actually, I'm *not* okay. I have some pretty difficult news to share with you."

I jumped up off the couch in a motion faster than I had moved in weeks and started heading toward the kitchen.

"What's going on?" I asked with sweating hands while I began pacing.

"The results of your CT scan are not indicating that anything is wrong with your gallbladder," he replied. "However, when we looked closer at the scan, we did see something, unlike anything we had ever seen before near your pancreas."

I couldn't breathe. My knees became weak, so I grabbed hold of the kitchen chair to keep myself from falling over while gripping my phone tightly in my other hand. My heart was beating so hard that I could feel the thumps in my chest as I anxiously awaited the next words he would say.

"We found a tumor, Nicole," he said in despair. "And the tumor is cancerous."

"What?" I asked, confused. "I have—cancer?"

The silence at the end of the line was deafening.

"Yes, Nicole," he said with great compassion. "We aren't entirely sure what type of cancer it is, but the way the light is reflecting off the tumor in the CT scan is showing us that you have some kind of cancer."

I folded my waist over the top of the chair that I was holding onto as I shuddered. I could barely grip my phone anymore with how weak I felt. I looked around as if someone would be there to catch me, but I was by myself.

"I have cancer?" I asked him again in desperation as if he could somehow change his answer.

"Yes," he said to me with his tone changing to one that was more serious. "Nicole, we need to get you in to see a surgeon immediately. Since it is already after 5:00 p.m., you'll need to call the number I am about to give you first thing in the morning to schedule an appointment. I'll let them know that this is urgent, and I will make sure that you are seen. Can you write this information down?"

"I can, I can," I stammered while attempting to move my arms and feet to grab something to write on. Tears filled my eyes. My body felt numb. I tried to move, but I couldn't.

"Nicole, are you still there?" Dr. Odekirk asked.

"Yes, yes, I am," I replied, choking out the words. "I'm trying. One second. I'm sorry. I'm sorry. I'm sorry."

"It's okay," he said to me with sympathy. "Take your time. I'll be right here."

I grabbed the first thing I saw. It was an envelope from a piece of mail in the kitchen. I hurriedly found a pen nearby to write with.

"Okay," I said while rubbing my eyes to try focusing. "I'm ready for the information."

With a violently trembling hand, I wrote down the name and phone number of the surgeon to call. It was nearly illegible from my shaking hand and was sprinkled with tears, which made the letters and numbers bleed together.

"Thank you," I said to him while covering my mouth and plugging my nose to keep from erupting with tears.

"I'll be in touch," Dr. Odekirk said. "I'll also be praying for you."

God, you say you keep track of every tear. You say that you will never leave me. You say that you love me. I'm looking for a light. I'm leaning into you.

Dear God, please, please help me through this. I'm truly afraid.

4

Hope and Heartache

Silence. All I could hear was the beating of my heart, the sniffling of my nose, and the shaking within my breath. I felt very alone.

It was as if I were standing outside of my body watching a movie of myself playing out, except I couldn't change the channel and couldn't turn it off. This was all happening.

Tears kept falling repeatedly down my face, plinking onto the floor. My brain began fogging with what seemed like hundreds of thoughts.

I have what? How? I'm only twenty-seven years old. I was on a beach in Hawaii one month ago and I was fine. I'm so confused. What are we going to do? Barely anyone knows I'm even sick. How am I going to tell them?

I tried to sit down but the second I made contact with a chair I was back up again, vigorously pacing around the kitchen table.

Until this point in my life, I had defined "cancer" as a disease *someone else* had. I had to completely redefine that word with one five-minute conversation. I didn't think I was immune to it, but it had never been something I had dealt with. I guess I never thought I would.

But sure enough, it was true. There I stood with cancer.

"Breathe, Nicole," I said out loud while taking short inhales and exhales through pursed lips. I scanned the empty house. "*God, I need you. I might feel alone, but I'm not alone. You're with me right now. I know you are. I'm scared, but I know I can trust you. Help me.*"

I closed my eyes and slid both of my hands down my face. I wanted to wipe off the layer of fear that had covered me and replace it through courage and hope.

After taking a few more deep breaths, I picked up the phone to call Wes.

Please answer, please answer.

"Hey, Nikki," he said into the phone with anticipation in his voice.

I instantly burst into tears. Wes had been my safe place, confidant, comforter, and best friend for years now. I couldn't believe that I was about to tell the one person I loved more than anyone in the world that I had been diagnosed with cancer.

"Honey," I managed to mutter, "the doctor said I have cancer."

And then there was a moment of silence. He held my vulnerable heart in his hands as I served up devastating news. I could hear him breathing forcefully and I wondered what he was thinking.

"Oh, Sweetie, I love you," he said to me quietly. "It's going to be okay. I am so sorry that I am not there with you right now. I don't even have words. All I can think to do is to pray."

> *"O Lord God, you are gracious and loving. We need you now, Jesus. Please have mercy on Nicole. Please have mercy on her. Please bring healing to her body. Please remove this cancer. No matter what comes next, we know that you will walk through this with us. Be with her now, Lord. In Jesus's name. Amen."*

"Thank you," I cried on the opposite end of the phone.

"I'm coming home right now," he insisted.

"No, Wes," I said to stop him. "It's okay, really. You're off in less than an hour. I'm okay. I'll be okay. Just come home when you're finished with your shift. I'll be here waiting."

"I love you," he said fiercely. "I promise the moment I arrive I'll not leave your side. We're in this together."

After he spoke those beautiful words, he told me he would be home soon and we ended the call. I walked toward the window and looked at an outside world that had no idea what was going on behind these closed doors.

As I lifted my gaze, I saw light shining through scattered gray clouds. I realized that this terrifying diagnosis had limitations on what it could do to me. The future was unpredictable, but cancer couldn't stop our prayers or take away the love of my loyal husband.

I was up against a ruthless competitor, but I was ready to discover and capitalize on every possible opportunity to run cancer into the ground.

I heard the front door open. Wes was finally home.

My stomach was hurting worse than before, but I desperately began taking slow steps toward the door to reach him. I heard a thud of equipment hit the ground followed by quick, heavy footsteps growing louder in my direction.

"I'm here," he panted as he scooped my weakened body up into his arms. "I'm here. I'm here. I'm here."

I melted into his embrace and buried my tear-soaked face into his chest.

"In sickness and in health," he restated from the vows he had made to me three years ago. "Until death do us part."

With almost no delay I began sobbing heavily. My tears were filled with equal parts devastation from the diagnosis and gratitude that he was here.

After a few moments, I nodded my head as a silent thank you and motioned gently to be released from his arms.

"What are we going to do?" I choked the question out of my mouth.

"We're going to take this one day at a time," he said to me as he held my arms and looked intently into my eyes. "We'll do whatever it takes. God will be with us. You will not fight this alone."

"I believe you," I replied in a haze.

And then it dawned on me.

"Babe," I continued with a shaking voice. "How are we going to tell everyone? I could be going into surgery tomorrow. I don't even know where to start."

"It's okay," Wes said to me, sensing the panic in my voice. "We can make calls together."

The next six hours were some of the most difficult conversations I had up until this point in my life. We made phone calls and sent text messages telling the news to everyone we loved. We also told each person that I would be seeing a surgeon tomorrow and could be having surgery by the end of the day.

My head and heart felt as if they might burst from the replies that came through about my diagnosis:

"No, no, no," a friend cried as she had recently lost a loved one to cancer. I knew it was like hearing my death sentence when I shared the news.

"It's probably just your gallbladder," a family member replied, optimistic and hopeful that it wasn't cancer.

"You can't die," another person said to me lovingly as she was convinced of this truth. "You're too nice and the world needs you."

"I don't know what to say except that I love you," a loved one said with numbness in her voice.

Tremendous shock, countless questions, exploding tears, moments of silence, and searing fear crossed the sound waves and screens of our phones for hours upon hours. Some tried to make jokes, others rerouted the conversation, and many told me why I was likely diagnosed with cancer. I had friends pray with me over the phone who had never prayed with me before and others who couldn't speak at all.

I was weary, foggy, and exhausted.

I prayed quietly under my breath:

> *Thank you for the people you have brought into my life to journey with me through this diagnosis. Help me to abound in love. Please help everyone, including me, process through this news and find hope in you.*

When I lifted my head, Wes was standing next to me smiling with his hand moving to my shoulder.

"We're going to get through this," I said to him with determination. "Cancer may be something I have, but I refuse to let it destroy my spirit."

5

Rollercoaster

My head pounded from the alarm clock sounding the following morning to wake me up.

Was it all just a bad dream?

The intensity of my headache and the continued pain in my abdomen reminded me that this was all happening. Wes had already gotten out of bed and I could vaguely hear him downstairs on the phone. We were instructed to call the surgeon's office at 7:00 a.m. so I had assumed that was who he was on the phone with. I then heard footsteps running up the stairs.

"Good morning, love," Wes said as he caught his breath and kissed my forehead. "The surgeon can see you at 7:30 a.m. this morning. I think it's just a consultation, but it could be possible that surgery will happen today. How can I help you get ready?"

"Good morning," I said groggily, still trying to wake up. "If you could just throw some overnight clothes into a bag for us just in case I have surgery, that would be great. I'll put on my sparkly boot and start getting ready."

Without having time to think or talk, we went through the motions quickly to get to my appointment. I strapped my orthopedic boot onto my foot and hobbled downstairs to get into the car.

"What's on your mind?" he asked me when we began the drive.

"Besides having my wisdom teeth out, I've never had surgery," I shared honestly. "I usually pass out when it comes to needles. I can't imagine what this is going to be like."

"Having had multiple surgeries myself, I know it can be scary," he said to relate with me. "I can tell you what's encouraging was watching my body recover from it. The surgery takes some time to heal from, but our bodies are amazing in how they repair themselves."

"They might not even have to give me an anesthetic because I might pass out when they put the IV in," I joked nervously after we parked and started heading toward the clinic.

"If you do have to have surgery, I'll make sure they give you the anesthetic even if you pass out," he said as he gave me a little squeeze on the arm and winked.

When we entered the waiting room of the surgeon's office, we noticed that it was covered in baseball memorabilia. Photographs of famous baseball players lined the walls throughout the office. Since I liked to pace when critically thinking, it made for a great excuse to circle the waiting room to look at the photos to pass the time.

"We received all your records and scan images from Dr. Odekirk's office," the medical assistant shared with us as she took us back to the patient room. "Dr. Barnes is wonderful, and he'll be in shortly."

"Thank you," I said as she exited the room.

Everything felt incredibly real now as we sat in the room and waited. I stared blankly at more signed photographs on the white walls of the room and zoned out. The thin white paper that covered the patient's chair started to dissolve underneath my legs as I was sweating profusely amidst my thoughts.

I heard footsteps approach the door and my attention fixated on the turning door handle. Dr. Barnes walked into the room with a smile on his face.

"Hi there," Dr. Barnes said to both of us and shook our hands. Within the first few moments he was in the room, he had been incredibly kind. His love for baseball was apparent with the décor and we could see his heart for his patients in the way he spoke with us.

He crossed his arms and had a look on his face as though he was thinking and searching for a way to communicate his next words to us.

This was the moment we were waiting for—to find relief, direction, and to discover the help that I desperately needed.

"I'm not convinced that this is cancer," Dr. Barnes said.

What did he just say? In baseball terminology, that news is definitely a curveball. I know I must be dreaming now.

I just stared at him. I was overwhelmed and massively perplexed. My mind was overflowing with countless questions. The remaining paper underneath me was now fully stuck to my legs, and my hands were shaking.

This could be great news—although we had just reached out to everyone we knew less than twelve hours ago and told them that I had cancer. Had we just scared everyone for no reason?

He said the symptoms I was experiencing are typically the side effects of a failing gallbladder. He then proceeded to share with us the additional testing he wanted to do to learn more about both the tumor and my gallbladder before moving forward with a surgery.

Wes held my clammy hand tightly and nodded at me. He was nonverbally reassuring me that he had heard what Dr. Barnes said and that we were going to figure this out. I was thankful for Wes being there because I couldn't keep my mind focused and I certainly wouldn't remember everything that was said.

"Okay," I replied and thanked him for his time. "Let the scans begin. We have some phone calls we need to make, too."

"Yes, we do," Wes said, taking my hand to leave the clinic.

I couldn't change my circumstances at the time, so I could either have a spirit of defeat or a spirit of hope. I knew my attitude would be important through this and I kept telling myself that we were going to get through it.

It felt like I was playing in a baseball game like the pictures in Dr. Barnes' office. It was almost like I was standing at the plate with continual fastballs and changeups being thrown at me. I was swinging as hard as I could just to stay in the game but I was wearing out quickly. The best part about baseball, though, is that it's a team sport. I wasn't in this alone. There was no way that I was giving up either.

Cancer or not, we were on the way to figuring out what was going on with me.

6

Uncharted Waters

"Nicole," Libby said as we sat down to meet for coffee, "what a week you've had!"

It had been a week since I met with Dr. Barnes and completed the scans he had ordered. I had called my mentor, Libby, to see if we could meet at a local coffee shop so I could see her and update her on what all had happened.

Over the last several years, Libby had mentored me. We had worked together at a church and then she had stepped into my life and guided, challenged, encouraged, and uplifted me in my faith. We had grown so close that she was like a second mother to me.

"It feels like things are happening quickly and at an excruciatingly slow pace all at the same time," I said to her in full exhaustion. "I can't believe it's July. It's hard to grasp that this is all happening."

"Can you walk me through your tests results again?" she asked while thoughtfully pulling out her journal where she took notes of our conversations together.

"One test showed that my gallbladder is failing so I'm scheduled for surgery to have it removed," I shared with her. "Dr. Barnes believes my gallbladder is what has been causing all my pain and discomfort in the last three years. He's the first doctor who ordered the correct scan I needed to find that out."

"So is it possible that the tumor is not cancerous and not harmful?" she asked.

"It is possible," I replied. "The back and forth of 'You may have cancer' and 'I don't think you have cancer' has been giving me whiplash."

"You've been living with a lot of unanswered questions," Libby said to me as she took a drink of her coffee. "The good news is that God is not surprised by any of this. He holds your future and He is working all things together for your good. He loves you. Moment by moment God will carry you through."

I held on tightly to the warmth of my coffee cup and her words. She could see the desperation in my eyes for the much-needed encouragement she shared. I reflected on how God had carried me through years of digestive problems, blessed me with a beautiful marriage, and how he wouldn't stop loving me now.

"I needed to be reminded of that today," I told her. "Thank you."

"What are the next steps?" she asked.

"In a couple of days Dr. Barnes will remove my gallbladder and the 'mystery tumor,'" I said, using my fingers as quotation marks.

"I'm thankful it's almost here," she said. "And if *I'm* thankful, I can't even imagine how thankful *you* must be."

"I am really hoping this helps me feel better," I replied.

We talked for a little while longer and caught up on what was going on in her life too. She had a heart of gold and brought peace and hope to my life every time we got together.

"Well, I hope you have a happy Fourth of July," she said embracing me with a hug while we wrapped up and said goodbye. "Know that this surgery will be over soon!"

"I'm forever grateful for you," I said while heading to my car to drive home.

The last few weeks had been draining. I felt like a hamster running tirelessly in its wheel going nowhere way too fast. Sickness increased alongside the number of questions I had. Family and friends reached out with kind words and prayers and it took every ounce of strength I had to reply. It felt as if I were falling apart in some ways.

When I arrived home Wes looked lively amidst his overtiredness.

"Have a seat, my lady," he said while pulling up a chair for me. "I want to read this to you."

He pulled out his Bible and opened up to a page he had bookmarked and read to me:

> *We are afflicted in every way, but not crushed; perplexed, but not driven to despair; persecuted, but not forsaken; struck down, but not destroyed; always carrying in the body the death of Jesus, so that the life of Jesus may also be manifested in our bodies. For we who live are always being given over to death for Jesus' sake, so that the life of Jesus also may be manifested in our mortal flesh. So death is at work in us, but life in you.* (2 Corinthians 4:8–12)

The words danced right off of the pages of Scripture and directly into my weary soul. Although I was feeling helplessly out of control, God lifted me back up, providing real hope for the journey through this scripture, Wes, and Libby. I was broken in many ways, but I wondered if this were a place where growth would happen, a place where I released control and fully trusted God.

"It's going to be okay, isn't it?" I asked him candidly.

"You know it," Wes said as he smiled at me. "We'll get through your surgery together."

"I believe you. We can do this."

I slowly opened my eyes. I was cold and alone, surrounded by white walls and bright lights. Everything was blurry from my contacts being taken out and I squinted, unsure of what was going on.

I had made it through my very first surgery.

My mom and Wes entered the room.

"Hey, you," my mom said, coming up beside me, tucking my hair behind my ear. She had flown up from Houston to stay with us so she could be here for my surgery.

"How are you holding up?" she continued.

"I'm doing fine," I replied. "I do feel pretty groggy, though. What happened during my surgery?"

"Surgery took about two hours," Wes informed me. "Dr. Barnes was able to remove your gallbladder successfully and you have only a few incisions in your abdomen."

"What about the tumor?" I asked with anticipation.

"Well, that's a different story," he began explaining. "He said there was less than a one-percent chance that the tumor is cancerous, so he removed as much of it as he could without disturbing your pancreas. He said anytime surgery is performed close to the pancreas it can be risky."

I was still pretty groggy and faded back to sleep. After some time had passed and I woke up again, I could feel the abdominal pain creep in. Since I began to gain lucidness, I revisited the question I had asked before.

"So there's still part of this tumor inside of me?" I asked for clarification.

"Yes, there's still part of it inside of you resting on your pancreas," he said. "The portion that he removed was almost the size of a baseball."

"Wow, that's huge! I'm hopeful that this fixed the problem and will help me feel better. I've been desperate for relief. Thank you both for being here with me."

"We wouldn't be anywhere else," Wes replied on behalf of him and my mom.

Wes didn't leave my side the entire time I was in the hospital. He slept in a chair next to my bed, helped me get up in the middle of the night to use the restroom, and walked the halls with me. I was grateful for his loyalty and that the pain I was in was a "healing pain" rather than one of suffering.

When I was finally cleared to be discharged from the hospital, Kathy and Bode let us borrow their recliner so I could sleep sitting up. The activities I could do were limited, but Wes and my mom got creative and purchased board games so I could be entertained in recovery.

I felt surrounded by love and hope. I was finally able to eat food again, confirming that my gallbladder had been the culprit causing problems for me. Friends came to visit and would bring treats, cards, and Disney-themed puzzles since everyone knew how much we loved Disney.

But one question loomed over our heads like a dark cloud following us around. It was a question we would have to face soon and it could change the course of our entire life.

Did I have cancer or not?

7

It's Official

My mom returned home to be with my dad, where they continued to unpack and settle into their new home in the Houston area. I couldn't tell if it was harder for my mom or for me to say goodbye. It had finally sunk in that they had moved away for good. I wished I had been able to see my dad too. I missed having them and their golden retrievers close by since puppy kisses were like medicine for my soul.

Twelve days had passed since my surgery. We finally had an appointment scheduled early in the morning with Dr. Barnes to go over the pathology results of the tumor. The anticipation came over me like a tidal wave that would take my breath away without notice. Wes had taken such great care of me and talked me through every moment of stress I experienced.

After gently helping me into the passenger seat, Wes walked over to the driver's side of the car to get ready to drive us to my appointment. Although I had already begun to heal, my mobility was slower since my core was unstable and sore from surgery. It was my first day to be without my sparkly boot since I had rested my foot through recovery. Wes reached over and pulled the seatbelt across the pillow that I held on my stomach, buckled me up, and then we headed to see Dr. Barnes.

He dropped me off at the front of the hospital where Dr. Barnes' clinic was located. It was only 7:00 a.m. so there weren't many people around. After Wes had quickly parked the car and made his way toward me, we headed upstairs to my appointment.

"Thank you for seeing us this morning," I said, thanking Dr. Barnes' medical assistant.

"It's not a problem," she told us kindly as she brought us back to the patient room. "Dr. Barnes wanted to see you before he went into surgery today."

"Good morning," he said to us upon entering the room. "We have received your pathology results, Nicole."

He stood across from me and leaned up against the sink in the room with his arms folded in front of him much as he did the last time we saw him. He seemed distraught, though, which was uncharacteristic from our last visit with him.

"What did the report say?" I asked him while my voice cracked.

"The pathology shows that you have what is called sarcoma cancer," he began.

"It *is* cancer?" I asked him as I felt my body go numb.

With his head tilted down toward the floor, he shifted his eyes up toward me and slowly nodded.

"What is that?" Wes asked, insistently shifting to the edge of his chair. "I've never even heard of that."

"It's very rare," he said. "Fewer than one percent of people are diagnosed with it. It was described to me as 'angry,' 'aggressive,' and 'high grade.' I'm so sorry to have to be the one to tell you this news."

It began feeling as if the walls of the room were closing in and the oxygen was being sucked out. I panted a few times and without even realizing it I had stood up.

"I just need a moment to breathe in the hallway if that's okay," I said motioning my hand toward the door.

"Absolutely," Dr. Barnes replied. "Please take your time."

Wes quickly stood up next to me to follow me out into the hallway, but I gently shook my head.

"Are you okay?" he whispered.

"I want to catch my breath," I whispered back. "Will you be okay if I take a moment to be by myself?"

"Of course, Sweetie," he said to me, rubbing my shoulder. "I'll be right here. Take your phone and call me if you want me to come out there with you."

"Thank you," I told him, kissing him on the cheek. I stepped into the hallway to breathe and process the news. I held my abdomen and slowly walked back and forth through the empty corridor.

"Aggressive," "angry," and "high grade" are how he described it. That's pretty horrifying. Less than one percent of all cancer diagnoses? Well, now it makes sense why the radiologist and my doctors have never seen anything like it.

How am I not crying right now? Maybe the shock has absorbed my tears. Maybe since this is technically the second time in a month for me to be "diagnosed with cancer" I don't believe him. Maybe it's because I can't even remember the name of the cancer he just told me I have!

I have a million thoughts and a myriad of questions. Since Dr. Barnes didn't take all of the tumor out in my surgery, this means that the cancer is still inside me. What's going to happen next?

I immediately stopped and thought about the scripture Wes had read to me before my surgery. I was thankful to have my phone so I could pull it up and read it.

> *We are afflicted in every way, but not crushed; perplexed, but not driven to despair; persecuted, but not forsaken; struck down, but not destroyed.* (2 Corinthians 4:8–9)

I took a few deep breaths and leaned up against the wall as I noticed someone walking to a room past me. I glanced back at the verses and felt calm enough to go back inside to meet Wes. Dr. Barnes had stepped out of the room so it was just the two of us for a moment.

"Hey," he said while pulling me in gently for a hug, swaying me back and forth. "What do you need from me?"

"Can you tell me the name of the cancer I was just diagnosed with?" I embarrassingly asked since I couldn't remember.

"It's called sarcoma cancer. I don't recommend searching the Internet about it. Let's just focus on what Dr. Barnes tells us we need to do next."

I could tell by the look on his face that he had searched the Internet about my diagnosis and did not like what he had discovered.

Dr. Barnes knocked on the door to reenter.

"Come in," I said.

"What are the next steps for Nicole?" Wes asked in anticipation to learn my treatment plan.

"Well, it looks like you'll need another surgery," he began in a solemn tone. "The surgery is called 'the Whipple procedure.'"

"Could you explain to us what that entails, Dr. Barnes?" Wes asked as he placed his hand on my knee.

"It requires the removal of the head of your pancreas, part of your small intestine, and your gallbladder, which we already removed," he explained. "The reattachment of the small intestine to the pancreas is very complex. You will also have a full reroute of your bowels."

"Okay," I said, looking at Wes while gripping my pillow to my abdomen and chewing on my bottom lip. "Is this something you're able to do?"

"I've done it only once before," Dr. Barnes said to us. "I would highly recommend that you have the procedure done by experts who specialize in sarcoma cancer and this procedure."

"Who do we need to see?" I blurted out in desperation. "Where do we need to go? I'll do anything."

"Sarcoma cancer is very rare and there are few oncologists in the country who specialize in it," he explained. "But there *is* a place I know could help you."

"Where?" Wes asked with vigor.

"There are three major cancer centers in the United States that I can think of that would be helpful for your case," he said to us. "There is one specifically in Houston called the MD Anderson Cancer Center. Is it possible that you could make that work?"

"Houston?" I repeated as a question while I covered my mouth with my hand. "In light of recent events, I believe we can make that work. I just need to make a quick phone call to my parents, since they just moved there about a month ago."

Wes held my hand and shook his head while smiling. We were continually encountering opposition, but each time it had been met with something that brought us hope. The scripture that Wes had read to me reigned true. Even though I was afflicted, I was not crushed. Amidst feeling perplexed, I was not driven to despair. I may have felt struck down, but I was far from being destroyed.

I squeezed Wes' hand, nodded back at him, and called my parents.

Even in life's scariest moments, God was still working in the midst of it all.

Why do I ever doubt him?

8

Relocating

The waiting and the tossing and turning at night were finally met with an answer: I had cancer.

Not only did I have cancer, but it was extremely aggressive and would require a life-altering surgery. It felt ironic as I would try to calm myself before being diagnosed by saying, "Oh, Nicole, you're letting your mind run wild. It's probably not going to be nearly as bad as you imagine." As it turns out, the diagnosis had been far *worse* than what I had imagined.

I had to remind myself that even though my diagnosis wasn't good, we had a plan. God had revealed his love and grace to us in a spectacular way through my parents' move and the ability for us to move in with them so I could receive treatment in Houston. I believed God was with us and would continue to be with us every step of the way.

"I'm coming with you," Wes had said to me after Dr. Barnes gave the recommendation to be seen at a center center in Texas.

I looked at him with eyebrows raised and hope-filled eyes. For the first time that day, tears streamed down my face.

"I will never leave your side," he continued saying as a promise to me.

Things began moving quickly after that. Although we decided to take the leap in going to Houston together, we hadn't fully thought through how we were going to make it work financially. Although bills would still need to be paid, we were determined to stick together no matter what.

For better or for worse. We promised each other.

Neither of us knew or understood what challenges were up ahead, but we tried to remain focused on the things we could control.

For starters, we had quite a few phone calls that we needed to make to update family and friends with my official diagnosis. I took time to answer as many questions as I could and promised each person I spoke to that I would give everything that I had to beat this cancer.

One of my closest friends from college, Meagan, called me back almost immediately after we got off the phone.

"What's your bank account number?" she asked me, getting straight to the purpose of her call.

"Meagan," I replied, laughing, "what do you need that for?"

"I want to set up a fundraiser page for you since both you and Wes will be down in Texas without work," she explained. "This will help you pay your normal bills as well as any medical bills that you incur."

Her dad had passed away from brain cancer while we were in school together. I knew exactly what she was thinking by setting this funding page up: She wasn't going to lose another person she loved to cancer—not without a fight.

"I can't believe your willingness to set this up for us," I told her with great gratitude. "This will help us out tremendously, but you know I never would have asked anyone to do this."

"I know—which is why I didn't ask. I just requested your information."

It was hard to ask people for help. Sometimes I didn't know what to ask for and other times I held back because I didn't want to be a burden to anyone. But friends and family continued stepping into action for us. It made me realize just how important community is and the beauty of people's willingness to help.

Our employers were also incredibly understanding when we told them the news of my diagnosis. Both places of employment told us that we would have jobs when we returned.

After verifying that the MD Anderson Cancer Center took my insurance, we were able to schedule our first appointment for the last day of July, which was less than two weeks away.

By the grace of God, we had everything we needed to go fight cancer in Texas.

Since the drive would take multiple days, we decided to leave sooner than later to get settled.

The next five days before we left were filled with many tears, emotional goodbyes, and overflowing amounts of paperwork. Before hitting the open road, we decided to stop in to see both Dr. Barnes and Dr. Odekirk's office staff to thank them, pray with them, and say goodbye. Dr. Odekirk was out of town but the ladies promised to let him know that we had stopped by.

When we had been on the road for a couple of hours, my phone rang. It was Dr. Odekirk.

"Nicole, I'm sorry I missed you when you stopped by the office today," he said. "I've been on a fishing trip for two weeks. I'm sorry to hear about your diagnosis. I know that must be hard."

"I appreciate you calling while you're on vacation to follow up with me," I told him. "We're driving to Houston right now for me to be seen at the MD Anderson Cancer Center for surgery."

"Dr. Barnes told me that you would be going down to Texas for the procedure," he said and then paused for a moment. "The main reason I called is that there's something I want to tell you that I didn't mention previously. It's important to me that you know."

"What's that?" I asked.

"I never shared with you what actually happened the day I received the results of your CT scan."

"What happened?"

"I was sitting in my living room and my phone notified me that I had an email. The email stated that your CT scan came back negative, which meant that the radiologist did not see anything of concern from your imaging that day."

"What?" I asked, hanging on his every word. "I'm confused. When you called me that day, you told me that they found a cancerous tumor. I remember *that* very clearly."

"I know," he said. "As I stared at my email that day, my stomach began turning. I ended up calling the radiologist to ask her to look at your scan again. When she evaluated the scan a second time, she told me there *was* a tumor there that she had missed when she first analyzed your scan."

"No way," I said in shock. "If you hadn't called to check with her, my cancer would have been missed altogether. We would have just removed my gallbladder, assuming that was the only thing that was wrong with me, and the cancer would have likely spread."

"Yes," he responded quietly.

"But you made the call," I said, now crying, in the passenger seat of the car. "You called and you saved my life. I wouldn't even have a chance if it hadn't been for the stirring in your stomach and you making the call."

"I believe God loves you and has a plan for you, Nicole," he told me. "We're sending our prayers for you in the journey ahead."

"Thank you," I said. "Thank you for everything you've done and for sharing this story of hope with me. It reminds me that God is moving in powerful ways."

I shared the story with Wes in amazement after finishing the call. I was entirely grateful to God for pressing on Dr. Odekirk's heart and for his responding to that nudge.

We kept witnessing miracles happening all around us: my parents' move to Houston, our jobs secured, my insurance accepted at the MD Anderson Cancer Center, a funding page set up, and now this story from Dr. Odekirk. They were these beautiful, seemingly impossible realities divinely orchestrated by God. I couldn't help but cry out to God in gratitude right there in the car.

With no idea of what the future held, we were assured that God held the future.

All that was left now was the long, winding road ahead of us. We felt fueled by God's love and courage with every hour we drove.

Cancer had no power over the Holy Spirit and the miraculous happenings. It was all too amazing not to write down. I decided I would journal every day through cancer so I wouldn't miss it: the hard times, the beautiful moments, and the many ways that cancer couldn't win. Documenting them would encourage me through surgery and recovery.

Even though the cancer inside me was growing quickly, hope grew rapidly within me too. I was ready to battle cancer—and I was determined to win.

9

The Underdog

Our bags were unpacked as we had finally settled in at my parents' house. They had moved to a suburb about an hour north of Houston tucked away in a little neighborhood that mirrored a small forest with towering trees and small deer prancing about.

We were enjoying spending time with them and being covered in golden retriever fur and kisses each day. It hadn't set in that I was there for cancer treatment since I had healed from my first surgery and we couldn't technically "see" the tumor. I was grateful that the surgery I had alleviated all of the pain I had experienced before. I was able to eat food again for the first time in years without getting sick. We were truly enjoying the days we had with my family.

However, it all became very real on the day of my first appointment.

It was the last day of July and my first day as a cancer patient in Houston. On the way to the cancer center, I didn't know how to process all the emotions I felt.

After some time of driving into the city, we finally saw the MD Anderson Cancer Center becoming visible on the horizon.

It was gigantic in height and massive in its breadth. The multitude of buildings ahead each displayed the words "MD Anderson Cancer

Center." It was the size of a small city by itself as it towered over the streets below. The largest building had many glass windows reflecting a brilliant blue from the sky and appeared to be fifty stories in height.

I felt overwhelmed as becoming a cancer patient had become an alarming reality.

Wes had looked over at me. He placed his hand on top of mine in my lap.

"I have an idea if you'd be up for it," he suggested.

"Of course," I responded, trying to calm my nerves. "What's on your mind?"

"Why don't we list the reasons we're here fighting for your life? I know how you like making lists to stay organized, so maybe this can help keep your thoughts structured as well."

"That's a good idea," I said as we got closer to the cancer center with every passing minute. "I think that will be helpful. Can I have a minute to gather my thoughts?"

"Sure. Take however long you need."

I took a few deep breaths in and out and rolled my neck around slowly in each direction. I shook out my arms and reached for a sip of water as I mapped out my thoughts in my head.

"We're here to make our best efforts to save my life," I answered broadly. "The more time I live, the more time I get to spend with you. We're able to be here because we've been given everything we need, such as support from family, insurance coverage, and a place to stay."

"I agree with all of that," he said. "Keep going."

"I have a purpose in life and this life is worth fighting for," I said feeling my anxiety fade. "God has demonstrated so many miracles, such as my failing gallbladder remaining undiscovered for three years in order to warn us at the exact right time when the cancer was discovered."

As the buildings were now nearly right on top of us, tears fell from my eyes. I was reaching to find perseverance and strength in my heart.

"Maybe we can make an impact here," I told him as I sought a deeper purpose. "I've never spent much time around cancer patients so I'm wondering if we can learn what their needs are and find ways to serve them."

"That's beautiful," he said as he turned on the blinker to find a place to park.

How he maintains hope and focus in these moments can come only from God. I've never met anyone else with such faith. He filled my heart with hope during one of the most frightening moments in my life. God, thank you for Wes.

Wes took my hand and we walked side by side toward the entrance of the cancer center. I stopped about ten feet away from the sliding doors and looked up at the building that loomed over us. It made me realize just how small I was.

As I analyzed the MD Anderson Cancer Center logo, I noticed that there was a red line through the word "cancer" as if to eliminate it completely. Their goal was the same as mine: to end cancer forever. I pushed my hair behind my ears and heard familiar words of truth in my head:

> *Little children, you are from God and have overcome them, for he who is in you is greater than he who is in the world.*
> (1 John 4:4)

I clutched Wes' hand signaling that I was ready to go inside, and we courageously walked closer to the front doors.

The motion sensor triggered them to open and a wave of cold air poured over us. This was it. In just a few steps I would officially become a patient of the cancer center. I took my first step through the front door and took a deep breath.

We did it.

I scanned the lobby trying to take it all in. The inside of the building was just as impressive as the outside. In the center was a large information desk surrounded by volunteers to help people find their way around. Arrows were leading to elevators, gift shops, coffee bars, and restaurants within the building. The finishes on the walls were calming and the large fish tank in the lobby was peaceful to stand by.

In front of me, behind me, beside me, and all around me were people who were sick, bald, covered with masks, or being pushed by a wheelchair. I saw individuals with visible scars and missing body parts.

Each patient who walked these halls had a similar goal in mind: *survival.*

After finding the correct elevator, we headed to the ninth floor, where my first appointment was scheduled. There was a large sign that read "Sarcoma Center" hanging above the waiting room that we walked toward to get checked in.

We were greeted with love and tenderness at the front desk. It was incredible to see that a rare cancer had an entire department dedicated to it. We were definitely in the right place. Sitting on the counter was a jar filled with yellow ribbons and bracelets.

"What are these for?" I asked one of the ladies checking us in.

"These are for you," she said as she took one of each and handed them to us. "July is Sarcoma Awareness Month, so we have bracelets and ribbons to help create awareness."

"Thank you," I said to her as Wes helped me put the ribbon onto my shirt. "It's kind of crazy because it took me a while to even remember the kind of cancer I was diagnosed with and now it's the awareness month for it. Trust me—I'm fully aware of what it is now!"

"Did you know that the color for sarcoma is yellow and the flower is a sunflower?" she asked me. "Bright, strong, and beautiful, just like you. Just give me one minute. I'm going to print you a wristband."

"Thank you," I replied and then turned to Wes. "I had no idea that cancers had colors and flowers that represented them. I also think the only awareness month I've heard of is Breast Cancer Awareness Month in October."

This was like a whole new world for me. One that I couldn't unsee, nor did I want to unsee. God was stirring within my heart a love for cancer patients and their families. I wanted to learn everything there was to know about sarcoma cancer and how to encourage others through treatment and it was only my first day.

"Your oncologist is Dr. Conley," the lady told me as she placed a black-and-white wristband onto my arm. "He is truly wonderful. Leslie is Dr. Conley's nurse and she'll get your vitals and take you back to a room shortly."

"Thank you," I responded, observing the band. "What is this medical record number for?"

"You'll get to know that number very well. It's your patient ID number. You'll need that number for every phone call you make up here and every appointment."

The seven-digit number would be fairly easy to memorize, but it certainly made me feel like a patient. I knew with the constant reminder of the wristband on my arm that I would need to continually remind myself that I was more than a patient so it wouldn't strip me of my identity as a child of God, wife, daughter, friend, and human being.

When Leslie called my name for us to head back, she quickly brought Dr. Conley in for an introduction. Dr. Conley took ample time in answering our long list of questions about sarcoma cancer. He was very intelligent and easy to talk to.

"Did you have any other questions I can answer?" he asked, looking at both of us.

"When will we be scheduling the surgery?" I inquired. I was surprised that we hadn't talked about the Whipple procedure at all during the appointment yet.

"This week I have ordered some blood work and scans for you," he explained. "After we overview the results with our team, we'll schedule you another appointment to talk about them and go over the next steps."

In the days that followed, the number of needle sticks, abdominal and full-body scans, and appointments I had made my head spin. Navigating the many floors and different buildings of the cancer center was like participating in a corn maze at a fall festival except that it was freezing and indoors. My arms and wrists were sore and my mind was discombobulated. Wes helped me remember information because my comprehension skills were at the lowest they had ever been.

When we had finally completed all the scheduled appointments around the cancer center, we headed to our appointment with Dr. Conley to go over the results.

After a short time in the waiting room, Leslie came out to take my vitals and take us back to the appointment room. When she left, Wes and I made predictions about when we thought my surgery would be scheduled.

"I think they'll schedule it for two weeks out," I guessed. "What do you think?"

"I'm going to go with three days," he stated boldly. "I want this tumor out of you. I wish it could have been removed yesterday."

It had been hard for Wes not to be able to fix this. He desperately wanted me to be cancer-free and said he wished it was he instead of me who had been diagnosed, but we both knew it didn't work that way. He would do anything it took to get me to a cancer-free diagnosis.

Dr. Conley came into the room and greeted us kindly. I was nervous and excited. I wanted to get this over with, but I was horrified by the intensity of the surgery that was coming. He sat down in the chair in front of his computer, crossing his ankle over his knee, and began explaining the next steps.

"For each patient, a panel of providers within the Sarcoma Department come together to review blood work and scans to find the best treatment plan for that individual. Upon reviewing your case and results, our team recommends that you undergo six cycles of chemotherapy, a little over a month of radiation, and then have the Whipple procedure."

We were both way off on our guesses.

"Oh," I said in shock. I was not expecting him to say that.

"This treatment plan will give us the best chance at eliminating the cancer and keeping it from metastasizing or recurring," he explained.

"How long will all of that take?" Wes asked to help us better understand the timeline.

"The treatment and recovery will likely take around nine months. But things can change, and treatment could be slightly longer or shorter. That is what we predict, though."

I just stared at him. I needed a shovel to pick my jaw up off the floor.

Chemotherapy? Radiation? Surgery? Nine months?

Wes was writing down every word Dr. Conley said as fast as he could to help us keep up with it all.

"We need to begin treatment very soon," Dr. Conley continued. "Since sarcoma is aggressive, we will need to start your chemotherapy treatments within the next week."

"Okay, I can do that," I agreed without fully processing what I had just committed to.

I didn't know a lot about chemo, but every movie I saw and every picture I looked at made it look like a nightmare's nightmare. I had lost loved ones to cancer and remember them being incredibly sick and hospitalized, often unable to care for themselves.

There was also one other quality that each of them shared.

"Am I going to lose my hair?" I looked up at him, anticipating his answer.

"Yes. You will likely lose all your hair by the second cycle of chemotherapy."

I had been growing my hair out for over ten years. It was the only thing that made me feel secure in my skin since I had gained a lot of weight.

I knew I had the option to say no to chemo treatment, but the answer to me was obvious to say yes. I had a decision to make and I believed that my life was more important than my hair.

"Whatever it takes to stay alive," I said.

"I have two other appointments I would like you to go to before your first chemotherapy," he continued. "You will need to have a CVC [central venous catheter] line placed. It is a catheter placed in your body that will stay with you during the length of your treatment. It will help with blood draws and chemo administration to protect your veins from overuse."

"That sounds great," I replied, touching my sore arms and hands from this week of appointments without having a CVC line. "What else will I need to do?"

"Since you're both young, I would also like to get you set up with a fertility specialist here to discuss the effects that chemo has on fertility and your options regarding it."

"CVC line insertion and fertility appointment," Wes repeated back to Dr. Conley while overviewing the notes he had been writing down.

"That's correct," Dr. Conley replied. "Did you have any other questions for me?"

"I have one more," I responded. "Why did you choose to be a sarcoma oncologist?"

"When I learned about the rareness and the low number of treatment options available for sarcoma, I knew I wanted to specialize in it," he said confidently. "I wanted to fight for the underdog."

What a good-hearted man Dr. Conley was! He had purposely chosen sarcoma because of the difficulties this type of cancer brought. He wanted to make a difference. After hearing his answer, I knew we had chosen the right oncologist and team to aid me in the fight for my life.

"Thank you for fighting for everyone like me," I said as tears welled up in my eyes. "I'm so grateful you're on my team."

Everyone loves an underdog victory. I was determined to be one of them.

10

The Scalpel

"When does the anesthesiologist come in?" I asked eagerly from my inverted position on the hospital bed.

Two days had gone by since our appointment with Dr. Conley and I found myself at the first of two follow-up appointments before I could begin chemotherapy. At this appointment, I was having a catheter placed in my chest at the Wound Care Clinic located inside the MD Anderson Cancer Center. This was incredibly important so I could receive chemotherapy and have blood drawn without having constant needle sticks risking damage to my veins or other tissues.

To prepare me for the procedure, I removed my clothing from the waist up and had a large blue tarp placed over my body stretching above my head. The only place visible on my body was a square cut-out in the tarp beneath my clavicle where they would be placing the CVC line.

"There is no anesthesiologist," the nurse replied to me. "You'll be awake during this procedure."

"Please tell me you're joking," I begged.

I had been expecting to be asleep by now. There was not enough time for me to mentally prepare for having a hollow tube lodged into my chest while I simply laid there wide awake.

My head began sinking further as the nurse lowered me at a deeper decline.

"It's happening again," I said with a quivering voice while halfway laughing.

"What's wrong?" the nurse said as he stopped moving the bed down.

"I just started sweating and I can feel the paper underneath me dissolving," I said as he looked at me with concern. "No need to worry—it's kind of my thing these days."

"You're going to do great," he reassured me. "Your husband is going to a training session in a room right around the corner to learn how to help dress and clean the line after it's placed."

"What does that entail?" I inquired.

"It is a step-by-step sterilization process where he'll learn how to clean your line, sterilize it, reapply the dressing, and flush it," he explained. He could see in my face that I was slightly overwhelmed with this information.

"I don't want you to focus on all of this now though," he continued. "Just know that he's a good man for learning how to do this. Not everyone's caregivers are willing or able to learn how to do that. Because he's getting qualified, you won't have to come to the hospital every week to have it done here.

I cleared a lump in my throat and nodded my head. I appreciated what Wes was doing but I wish he would have been allowed in the room with me during the procedure. Feelings of gratitude and terror intertwined astoundingly often these days.

This is all in a great attempt to save my life.

"I'm happy to play any music you'd like," the nurse said to me. "Do you have a preference?"

"Worship music, if that's okay," I requested with my head halfway concealed from the tarp as I turned it toward the center of the room.

“Of course,” he said as he started the music and turned the volume up on the computer.

Because of my positioning, I could see only the lower half of his body moving while he continued setting up the room. I heard another set of footsteps join in the movement, but I couldn’t tell who it was quite yet.

When she spoke, I could tell by her voice that she was a woman. She moved quickly and with purpose. She was very direct and to the point when she spoke with the nurse as well.

“Hello,” I heard her say as she pulled up a chair in my line of sight. She took a moment to introduce herself and tell me a little bit about what she was going to be doing.

“Before we get started, I do want to remind you of the small percentage of people whose lungs collapse after this. I’ll just need you to stay calm, listen to the music playing, and focus on breathing slowly. I’ll walk you through every step.”

“I think I can do that,” I told her through a half-hearted commitment.

Since I was diagnosed with a cancer that fewer than one percent of people who are diagnosed with cancer get, percentages didn’t affect me. Anything over zero percent made it a possibility now in my book.

“Let’s get started then,” she said. She slid her chair away from me where I could no longer see her. I decided it would be best if I closed my eyes anyway.

“We’re going to start with injections to numb the area around your chest. You’ll feel a few stinging sensations.”

I took a sharp breath through clenched teeth. My eyes squeezed closed even tighter.

Ouch, ouch! Stinging sensation! Oh, that’s bad!

Again and again and again—it felt like ten injections had been used and the stinging was causing my eyes to water.

Listen to the music. Focus on my breathing. Step one is done. The numbing medication is sinking in. I’m almost numb. The rest should be all downhill from here.

She stepped away and I could hear her speaking with the nurse across the room while allowing my chest to numb. I hesitantly opened one eye to see if I could catch a glimpse of what was happening, and it seemed that they would be occupied for at least a few moments more. I was grateful to have more time to gather my composure and calm down before she got started.

How can I get through chemo if I can't get through this? This should be the least of my worries.

I tried everything I could to find a level head: I recalled all that God had done so far, sang along with the music, focused on my breathing, and even made jokes in my head. I was too panicked and everything I tried was tanking. I was headed straight into the storm.

Her footsteps loudened as she now was heading back toward me.

"Now we're going to insert the catheter," she told me. "You're going to feel some pressure."

"Agh," I groaned deeply while trying to keep my core still. I shifted my legs and kept grunting as it felt as if she were attempting to put a square peg into a round hole in my chest. It kept going and going, causing my entire head to start throbbing.

I let the music sink in. "Our God Is an Awesome God" was playing and I attempted to soak in the words with each forcibly slow breath I took.

Suddenly something didn't feel right. My head felt strange. I could tell something was very wrong.

"Is there ringing in your ears?" she asked me with a voice of urgency and concern. I opened my eyes and saw she had leaned her head down toward my face.

"There is," I said as I could feel my blood pressure rising. I felt my heart beating as though it were in the palm of my hands. For the first time in my life, I could feel blood pumping inside me.

"Is that supposed to be happening?" I whispered while trying to stay calm. "Is something wrong?"

"I believe the line routed up into her neck," she said, turning to the nurse. "We need to pull this out right now."

"Is something wrong?" I asked again while trying to control my escalating heartbeat. I had never felt so helpless. I wanted to jump up and run away.

"I need you to breathe normally," she said in a quiet and stern voice. "Don't talk. Breathe normally. Don't talk."

Are my lungs going to collapse? I feel as if my heart might explode. I think I'm going to be sick. Listen to the music. Listen. Breathe.

Our God is an awesome God.

I could feel the tube sliding through my chest and pressure slowly releasing as she carefully removed the catheter.

Our God is an awesome God.

Sing it slowly. Our God is an awesome God. Our God is an awesome God. Our God is an awesome God. Oh, lungs, please don't collapse.

"The catheter is out," I heard her report to the nurse.

"Thank you, Lord," I said as beads of sweat slid down my face and onto my pillow. I turned my head the opposite way toward the wall to try to loosen up the tension that had built up in my neck and shoulders.

"Are you ready to try again?" the nurse asked her almost immediately.

"Yes," she replied. "Can you get me the scalpel first?"

"Scalpel," I repeated, whipping my head back toward the center of the room with widened eyes.

I know that tool! Don't get that one!

Within moments I felt intense pressure on my chest. It made me want to be sick as I envisioned what was happening on the other side of the blue tarp. I thought I disliked *needles* more than anything until she asked for a knife. I wish I didn't know which tool she was using.

Couldn't she have used hand motions? Simply pointing to the tool would have worked. Or how about a code word? "Hey, can you pass me the gummy bears?" I don't think I would be panicking if I thought she was just having a mid-surgery snack. I know, I know. She's just doing her job. Oh, no—here comes more pressure.

What she did must have worked as the second insertion barely hurt at all, but my head was heavy from the adrenaline and stress. Breathing slowly was taking every ounce of strength I had left. I could feel her pull back and thought we might be finished.

"You did it," she said as she wheeled her chair back over to me. "He's going to put a couple of stitches in you to hold the line in place and you'll be on your way."

"Thank you," I said in a hoarse voice as my mouth felt as though I had eaten a bag of cotton balls.

The insertion of stitches in my chest was effortless compared to what I had just experienced. He covered the CVC line with a thick bandage and taped it on all four sides so I couldn't see what they had done. I put my clothes back on slowly so I wouldn't disturb the affected area on my chest.

It was incredible to be sitting up even though it felt as if I had been mauled by an animal. It was a miracle that my lungs hadn't collapsed during placement. I had never been so happy for something to be finished.

I was in a state of shock from the whole experience, and it was one of the very few times in my extroverted life that I did not want to speak.

In an attempt to stand up to meet Wes, I almost passed out. The nurse helped me into a wheelchair since I wasn't able to walk on my own yet.

"They should be finishing up the class that your husband is taking on dressing changes," he told me. "I can wheel you around the corner into that room so you can see him if you'd like."

"Thank you," I muttered.

When we arrived and the doors to the classroom opened, everyone turned around in their seats. There were about ten people in the classroom seated in rows watching a nurse give demonstrations on how to care for a CVC line on a mannequin at the front of the room.

Oh, so that's what the CVC line must look like on me.

It looked like a small purple triangle with wings coming off the sides of it that were stitched to the mannequin's chest. Through the center of the triangle was a hollow tube entering the chest from the top. The bottom was divided into two catheters that had clamps keeping them sealed until actively being used. Each tube had a cap on it. One was purple for chemo administration and the other was red for blood draws.

That was just placed in me. I think I'm going to be sick.

I looked away from it to try to find Wes.

He greeted me with a gigantic smile from across the room. He was even bouncing in his chair a little. I could tell he was excited to share with me all he had learned and that he had found a practical way to help. The nurse wheeled my chair through the center aisle and placed it next to an empty row where Wes moved back to sit in an end seat next to me.

"How did it go?" he whispered while the nurse continued to instruct in the front of the room.

I shook my head and stared blankly ahead. I couldn't even talk about it. I was not ready to relive it this soon.

"Are you okay? You look pale." He shifted toward me and placed his hand on my clammy forehead.

"I'm okay," I whispered back unconvincingly. "We might have to talk about it tonight or tomorrow."

"I understand," he said, turning his gaze back to the front of the classroom. "We're required to test out in front of the nurse before I'm allowed to care for your line at home and it's almost my turn. I'm excited that you get to watch."

Over the next few moments, I watched Wes in deep focus as he put to the test everything he had learned. I could barely move because I was so sore in my right shoulder, chest, neck, and back from the procedure, but I couldn't help but smile. Even though Wes couldn't be in the room with me during the procedure, he was out here doing everything he possibly could to help and love me well.

Cancer was already beating me up and I hadn't even started treatment. I wondered just how difficult this was going to be. I had never been tested and pushed past my limits like that. One thing the experience taught me already was that I could make it through hard things. As difficult as the procedure was, I hadn't told them to stop.

And I was going to fight through all six cycles of chemo too.

"Our God Is an Awesome God" helped get me through the procedure. The words reminded me of the unchanging truth that would continue lighting the way with each step I would take ahead.

After Wes passed his demonstration, I clapped softly for him by tapping my left hand on my thigh. He had already gone above and beyond to care for me, and I was in awe of his loyalty and dedication. Just a few months ago we were dunking each other in a resort waterpark in Hawaii, and now Wes was pushing me in a wheelchair toward the car as we left a cancer center.

Life had changed substantially, but his love hadn't changed at all.

Tomorrow we were scheduled to meet with a fertility specialist. I was tempted to be overwhelmed, but I found myself clinging to the words of Jesus:

> *Do not be anxious about tomorrow, for tomorrow will be anxious for itself. Sufficient for the day is its own trouble.* (Matthew 6:34)

These words had never reigned truer in my life than today. Today had brought plenty of trouble upon itself. Tomorrow could do the same, but there wasn't any need for me to worry about that now. Not a single hour of life would be added to mine by worrying. So when we arrived back at my parents' house I would focus on peace and rest.

The Lord knows I need it!

11

Fertility

"What are you thinking?" Wes asked me as we waited for the fertility specialist to enter the consultation room.

This appointment was undoubtedly different than the rest we had been to. Even the way the room was set up was distinctive. There was a round table with six chairs circled around it, which took up about half the space of the room. Posters hung on the walls displaying resources for fertility preservation, IVF (in vitro fertilization), and high-risk pregnancies. I was way out of my element.

"I'm glad that this appointment isn't to place a catheter on the opposite side of my chest," I joked with him whilst dodging his question. I shuddered even saying that out loud as it was still hard to talk about the CVC line insertion that happened yesterday.

"But really," he said trying to shift to a more serious conversation. "What do you think about all of this? What's on your mind?"

"I don't know *what* to think about it. You and I talked about waiting three to five years after getting married to have kids and we just celebrated our third anniversary a couple of months ago. It feels like we have to make a hard decision very quickly about something we've barely talked about."

"So much has changed in such a short time, and we're going to be having a pretty deep conversation about this subject today."

"I don't know what to expect," I said, leaning closer to him. "What if we don't even have time to make a choice? I start chemo in a few days."

"Whether they tell us we can have kids or not, we're going to make every moment of our lives together count," he said with tears welling up in his eyes. "Do you believe me when I tell you that?"

"I do," I said.

"Your continuing to stay alive is all that I care about right now," he told me with a very serious look on his face. "Your journey to beat this cancer and recover from it is my greatest dream for the future."

"Your love and understanding continue to amaze me," I told him. "I wish I could give you the world, but I promise I'll give you everything I have."

It was hard to think that we might learn difficult news. We weren't entirely sure if we wanted kids at that point, but we also weren't prepared to hear someone tell us that we never could. Psychologically, having that choice taken away would be heartbreaking.

The door to the consultation room opened.

"It's nice to meet you both," the doctor said, greeting us warmly. I could instantly read from her demeanor that her job often required the delivery of difficult news. She was careful and gentle in her words and movements. I couldn't even imagine the challenges of her job.

"I admire what you do," I spoke my thoughts into life as she looked at me, surprised.

"Oh, thank you," she replied, stumbling over her response to the unexpected compliment. I could tell that she was appreciative of the sentiment but could also see by her body language that she didn't have the best news to deliver to us.

"I would like to discuss your options regarding fertility," she began. "The options are limited with your case."

"Okay," Wes replied. "We're ready to hear them."

"Normally I would share a few options such as freezing your eggs, but we're out of time to do that," she told us with a saddened look on her face. "Your oncologist said you need to start chemo next week due to the location of your cancer and the aggressive nature of sarcoma."

"But you *did* say we had at least one option, right?" Wes asked, trying to lead the conversation in a positive direction.

"Well, yes, there *is* one option. Results aren't guaranteed, but there is an injection we can give you now and another one in three months during chemo. Essentially it will turn off the brain waves to your ovaries and could possibly protect them from chemo and radiation."

"Okay, that sounds like a good option," I said, jumping in and looking at Wes giving a quick shoulder shrug being halfway sold on the idea. "What are the side effects?"

"The most reported side effect is hot flashes," she said looking back and forth between us.

"How often do the hot flashes occur?" I asked her.

"It varies patient to patient," she replied. "One patient barely had any and another reported that she had hot flashes every ten minutes."

"Every ten minutes?" I repeated, enunciating every syllable to see if I had heard her correctly.

"That's correct," she said with a straight face.

"Wow!" I said gazing toward the floor while rubbing my hands slowly down my neck. "Can the two of us have a moment to discuss this?"

"Absolutely," she said understandingly. "I'll be right back."

She exited the room, closing the door slowly and softly.

We sat in our chairs around the empty table in silence, staring at each other, hoping that the other would speak first.

"Can you tell me what you're thinking?" Wes asked, breaking the silence.

"I don't know *what* to think," I said as unstoppable tears rolled down my face. I didn't even wipe them away as I thought maybe I could stop them from flowing if I ignored them. Unfortunately, that didn't work.

"Tell me about your tears," he inquired as he got up and stood behind me. He wrapped his arms around me gently so he wouldn't hurt my CVC line while pressing his cheek against mine.

"What do we do?" I whispered through now salty, tear-soaked lips. "We've never discussed this thoroughly—and now we have five minutes to make a decision that could affect our entire future."

I took a deep breath and decided to try verbalizing my thoughts.

"I could have over fifty hot flashes per day. This would be on top of any unpredictable side effects that come along with chemo. She said that this 'might work' without any statistics on the success rate of this treatment. However, if I don't have these shots administered, there is a chance that we won't ever be able to have kids biologically. I'm so torn and truly don't know what to do. What are *you* thinking?"

"This is heavy news," Wes said, pulling away from my face and shifting to kneeling in front of me. He tilted my chin toward him so he could look me in the eyes while brushing the back of his hand across my face to dry my tears.

"I need you to be alive," he said, placing both his hands on my legs. "It's the most important thing to me in the world. Let's focus on that and trust God with our future regarding children. He'll lead the way for us even if it looks different than what we thought it would."

"Thank you," I breathed out while rubbing my eyes. "I'm so sorry."

"What are you sorry about?"

"There is no way you signed up for this," I replied ashamedly. "You've already given up so much to be here with me and now I may never be able to bear a child with you or grow old with you."

"Hey—where is this coming from? This is *exactly* what I 'signed up for'—'for better or for worse,' 'until death do us part.' Do you remember those words that I said to you? I meant them then. I mean them now."

Wes held the pieces of my broken heart together as I fell apart in his arms. I couldn't believe that we were in a situation where in order to save my life, we would be potentially surrendering the ability for me to bring a child into his world. It was surreal. I felt a great heaviness and sadness within my soul.

"How am I going to get through this?" I asked him breathlessly in between sobs.

"*We,*" he emphasized as he dried my tears again, "*we* are going to get through this *together*. And on the other side of this, we'll find a way to have a child if it's God's will for our lives. There are other ways."

"Yes," I said tilting my head to the side. "I suppose there *are* other ways."

Even with the possibility that the long-term side effects of cancer treatment would keep me from bearing a child, there was still hope that we could have a baby in another way. It would likely look different than I had pictured, but I tried not to let it steal my joy. Wes' presence, wisdom, and love through today made me realize just how trusting he is of God's plan for our lives. His faith was inspiring.

Cancer had been the worst thing I experienced in my life thus far, but I kept finding that the brokenness and pain it was causing was not beyond repair. The hits were hard and heavy, but faith and hope were undefeated so far.

When the doctor came back in, we shared our decision with her. She ordered blood work for us so we would have a baseline of what my counts were before I started treatment and she said we would reassess when treatment ended. She was very understanding and wished us the best on our journey ahead.

"It will be good to visit Colorado this weekend before I start treatment next week," I told Wes as we pushed in our chairs and left the room.

"Indeed, it will be," he replied as we started heading to the car. "I think it will refresh and reenergize our souls in a beautiful way. When we get back you'll be ready."

I can't give up. I won't give up. My story isn't over yet. It's just getting started.

12

Perhaps

It was hard to believe that a weekend could come and go so quickly. Smiling faces and familiar places all felt so distant, so I tried to take in every moment. The early August air in Colorado started showing signs of fall with the breeze blowing a little bit cooler than when we were last there.

Twenty-four hours felt like a lifetime ago as the scenery of our lives had changed radically. I was back in Houston reclined in a hospital bed at the MD Anderson Cancer Center in a patient room at the Ambulatory Treatment Center for my first cycle of chemotherapy to begin. The sliding door had a green-and-white closed curtain giving Wes and me our own private space with each other for treatment. Wes sat in a chair next to the bed with his backpack full of games, books, and a fluffy blanket for me.

I would have chemo administered on two consecutive Tuesdays followed by one week off before beginning another cycle. This would repeat for six cycles resulting in a total of eighteen weeks of treatment. It was too big for me to grasp in its entirety, so I just focused on one treatment at a time.

While we waited for our nurse to hook me up to an IV bag, I reflected on the time we had just spent in Colorado.

I savored the long hugs from my in-laws. I sought wisdom and prayer from Libby. My friend, Jenna, and I daydreamed of planning a Disney vacation together when this was all over. We made great memories with friends and they all decided to name my CVC line “Carl” to make it less intimidating for me. Memories and selfies were the souvenirs I brought back to Texas with me to help keep me strong. It was exactly what I needed before starting chemotherapy.

It dawned on me that I had often taken precious moments like those for granted. I wish I didn’t have to have my world turned upside down to see things right side up. I vowed to cherish special moments like these from now on.

“How’s Carl doing?” Wes asked, interrupting my thoughts. “I know you loved having him at your blood draw this morning so you didn’t have to get your arm stuck with a needle.”

“Carl is still a little tender but is doing well,” I chuckled while placing my hand over my newly named CVC line. Naming it had taken away some of the trauma associated with the insertion.

“It was great to see everyone a few days ago,” I followed up while tucking the pink fluffy blanket around my torso. “It’s hard to believe we were just in Colorado and now I’m getting ready to have chemo in Texas for the first time.”

“You’re going to be great.” Wes grabbed our hospital bag and inched closer to me in his chair.

“This is all very surreal,” I said, breaking eye contact to make observations about our surroundings. “Here we are in this hospital room and I don’t even have any symptoms. I’m feeling better than ever since my gallbladder has been removed. I can’t see or feel this tumor and I’m willingly having medication injected into my body that is supposed to help me but is also going to make me violently ill and cause my hair to fall out in the process.”

My eyes met back up with Wes’ as I awaited his contributing

thoughts. His eyes lit up and he lifted his pointer finger in the air motioning at me to wait.

"Can I take a quick picture of you?" he asked, eagerly reaching into his backpack to grab my phone.

"That's an odd request," I said, laughing while he pulled up the camera app on my phone.

"Smile big," he said smiling as if he were in the photo himself. I glanced at him in confusion but obliged for a photo.

"Now look at it closely," he encouraged as he handed the phone over to me. "What do you see?"

I stared at the photo, trying to make sense of what he was up to, but his lips were sealed.

"Don't overthink it, honey," he responded, urging me to refocus. "I just want you to remember this. What do you see in the picture?"

"I look tired," I said as I zoomed in. I observed my drooping eyes from the lack of sleep from racing for weeks on end. "I see my CVC line coming out from the neckline of my shirt. I also see my pink fuzzy blanket peeking up at the bottom of the picture."

"What else?" he asked, encouraging me to look again. I could tell at this point that he wanted me to look beyond the obvious. He must have had a reason for this, so I was willing to accommodate his request.

"I see the words on my shirt 'Perhaps this was the moment for which you were created,'" I said with my eyes welling up with tears. "I'm trying to be brave, but I don't feel like I am."

"Do you believe those words?" he asked me.

"That this is the moment for which I was created?" I repeated to him in question. "Perhaps it *is.* I see a new passion welling up within my heart. I want to help people like me battling cancer. Maybe a new direction has been set before me. Maybe this is what I've been created to do."

"That's powerful, Nicole. I know you're going to make a difference in this world, but those are not the words I was asking if you believed."

"Oh?" I replied, looking up from my phone and shifting in my bed, fully facing him. "What *were* you asking?"

"Do you not feel brave?" he said with his head tilted down and his eyes lifted up toward me. "Look at the picture again. Look how far you've come."

I stared at the photo for a moment and then looked back up at him. I saw myself sitting in a hospital bed with a catheter coming out of my chest. Although exhaustion plagued my body, I had shown up for treatment. I was scared, but there was something inside me that was stronger than fear. Living was too important for me to back down from this fight.

"God, our family, our friends, and our team have all given me the courage to be here right now," I said in gratitude. "Thank you for reminding me of that this morning. Thank you for capturing it."

The sliding glass door and curtains began opening.

"Are you ready?" the nurse asked me.

"I am," I replied while locking eyes with Wes.

"This will take about ninety minutes," she said hooking me up to the IV line before she left and closed the door. "If you need anything, please let me know."

The bag that was filled with my chemo medication was pinned high up on the IV pole. It slowly began dripping into the line that led to my body. I gazed up at it, baffled that this medicine would both help me and hurt me. It seemed so backward, but I believed that my care team had the best intentions and treatment plan to help save my life. I trusted them.

As I watched the chemo fall and make its way through the tube attached to my CVC line, my body shivered. The medication felt cold entering my body. I quickly looked away because it was too much for me to watch. I knew if I allowed myself to overthink it, I could send myself into a spiraled panic. That would be the last time I watched the chemo drip into my line.

I closed my eyes and leaned my head back. My mind took me back to joyful times like our wedding day, our anniversary trip to Hawaii, and family meals. It had been a lot less complicated than things were now.

There was a hope harbored deep within my soul and a fierce fighter who had been discovered within me, though. I was reminded of my life verse:

> *I have told you these things, so that in me you may have peace. In this world, you will have trouble. But take heart! I have overcome the world."* (John 16:33, NIV)

Perhaps this was the moment for which I was created. Perhaps this journey would grow me in ways that I couldn't have grown without it. Perhaps I could live to tell the story.

"Are you doing okay?" Wes asked me, halting my thoughts. He had been reading but looked up to check in on me.

"I am," I replied, opening my eyes. "Other than my chest feeling cold, I can't even tell that I'm receiving chemo."

"You're doing great," Wes said as he closed his book and climbed up on the hospital bed with me.

We read and played card games for a while to pass the time. I could hear people walking around outside our room and the sound of IV poles being rolled as patients were able to disconnect them from the wall to go on a walk if needed.

After a while, I started feeling overheated. I pulled my hair up into a ponytail to try cooling off.

I realized it would be one the last times I would be able to do that for a long time.

The machine started to beep, and the nurse came back into the room.

"You're all finished," she said while disconnecting Carl from the IV line. We packed up the blanket and card games to head back to the car.

I had made it through my first chemo treatment. I was surprised that I wasn't instantly sick since that was how the movies portray it. My chest felt heavy and I was tired from all the apprehension that led up to it and being at the cancer center for a long time.

"You did it!" Wes exclaimed as we walked out toward the car. "How do you want to celebrate?"

"This might seem like a weird way to celebrate," I began replying. "But I want to schedule an appointment to have my head shaved."

Dr. Conley had told us that my next dose of chemo would be a combination treatment using two separate medicines. He said that the second week of each cycle would be the most difficult on my body since the combination included a more aggressive chemo. This was the medicine that was going to cause me to lose my hair.

"Well, we can schedule an appointment for *both* of us," he said. "I'll shave my head with you."

"That's considerate of you," I told him as we loaded up the car. "Let's make some phone calls and we can get it scheduled."

It was nerve-racking to think about shaving my head, but I knew it was what I wanted to do. I had spoken with patients in waiting rooms to gather recommendations of whether I should do that or let the chemo take it naturally.

While there wasn't a right or wrong answer on what to do, I wanted to educate myself on both sides to decide what was the right path for me to choose.

One woman shared with me that she woke up one morning with hair in her mouth that had fallen out the night before. Another woman said she cried while watching her long hair hit the floor in clumps while she brushed it. I even researched online and a blogger shared that she felt empowered shaving her own head since she felt she had lost control of so much already.

The decision was clear to me that having my head shaved was the way for me to go.

By the time we got back to my parents' house, we had set the date to say goodbye to my hair. In three days my bleached blonde highlights would fall to the floor.

At every turn, a new obstacle was in my path for me to face and this would be a very challenging one for me.

Brave. I needed to be brave.

13

My Hair

Hair. Over the years I had developed many thoughts toward it: There was too much of it when I was in a hurry to get ready, there wasn't enough of it when I wanted to style it the ways the models do, and I was frustrated when I felt it wasn't cooperating with what I wanted it to do.

My days ebbed and flowed with what I would consider good hair days, bad hair days, throw-it-in-a-ponytail kind of day, wear-a-hat-on-top-of-it day, and coloring it until it was bleached blonde.

One thing was certain: I had always been attached to the hair on my head, both literally and figuratively.

Beginning in my teen years, I began growing my hair out and decided that I would never cut it beyond a trim. I wanted it to be as long and as big as humanly possible. In short, "The bigger the hair the closer to God" was a motto I lived by. While that's not technically true, I certainly acted like that with my fixation on having big blonde hair.

Although it started as something easy to pull back in a ponytail for sports, it quickly became a crutch in my young adult life when I had gained a significant amount of weight. It was one of the only things I felt I had control over and made me feel pretty. When I felt I wasn't at the weight I wanted to be, I would hide behind my hair. Much like Linus's blanket in the Charlie Brown comics, my hair had become a security blanket.

I never thought there would come a time where I would have to cut my hair, much less lose it completely—and more than that, a season when I would lose all of it. Yet here I was. The sacrifice would be an exchange for the medication in an attempt to save my life, but it was still hard to do since I had invested time, money, and even part of my identity in it.

The day had finally arrived for me to shave my head. It had been three days since my first chemo, and I knew side effects would emerge soon. It was important for me to have my head shaved before I started feeling sick.

Wes and I drove up to the hair salon, parked, and walked inside. I was so nervous I couldn't stand still. My eyes wandered and observed the frosted white designs that spiraled across the windows in the front of the salon. The salon was filled with bright lights and positive energy from the stylists who worked there, which I desperately needed.

We checked in at the front desk and stood in the front doorway while we waited.

"Can we take 'before' and 'after' pictures?" I asked Wes so we wouldn't have to sit down.

"Of course," he said as he took my phone to snap a selfie of us in front of the beautiful designs on the glass.

"Are you Nicole?" I heard a woman ask as she came up around the corner.

"I am," I replied. "And this is my husband, Wes."

"Hi. It's nice to meet you both," she said in an excitable voice. "I'll be taking care of both of you today."

"Thank you," I said. "Both of us are going to shave our heads."

"When I spoke with Wes on the phone, he had mentioned that you were interested in shaving your head yourself," she described from their conversation. "Since it can be kind of tricky with longer hair, I would like to cut it down shorter first and then I can show you how to use the clippers to do the first official shave. Would that be okay with you?"

"Yes, that's fine," I said as she walked us back to her station. I could feel my palms begin sweating. "Can I run to the restroom really quick?"

"Of course," she replied, seeing that I needed a moment to myself. "We're in no rush."

I opened the door, stepped inside, and leaned up against the door. It was a single stall, so I had the room to myself.

The mirror was right in front of me as I looked ahead and stared at myself. I tried pulling my hair back into a tight ponytail and even covered my hairline with my hand, but it was impossible to picture what I would look like without any hair. It was hard to think I was pretty with this hair, so it felt impossible to think I could be without it.

I could hear myself breathing heavily. I walked forward and placed my hands on opposite sides of the sink. I bowed my head and closed my eyes to pray.

> *Dear God, I don't know what I'm going to look like without hair or how others will react when they see me. I know that chemo is trying to save me and that is why I have chosen to do this. Help me to find my identity in you. Help me to find my security in you. Help me to see myself in the same way you see me. You have seen how many years I have desperately held on to my hair and you see how hard this is for me to let it go. Please help me to love myself the way you love me. Please hold me close. I love you.*

After splashing water onto my cheeks, I stepped out of the bathroom and closed the door gently behind me. As I took steps toward Wes, he smiled at me with compassion. I sat down and held onto the arms of the salon chair while my hairstylist draped a pink hairdresser cape over my shoulders. Wes stood in front of me while leaning up against the large wall mirror, never breaking eye contact with me.

"Are you ready?" she asked with a cheery disposition as she flipped my hair back and forth. I looked ahead into the mirror since it would be the last time I would see my hair in a ponytail for a long time.

"I am," I replied.

Snip. Snip. Snip.

Within a moment nearly two feet of hair had fallen to the floor.

"You're beautiful," Wes mouthed to me with an ever-widening smile.

With all the anxiety and pressure that had built up to that moment, I was surprised that I hadn't cried yet.

"Now it's your turn," the hairstylist said to me and handed me the electric trimmer. "You're ready for your first official head shave."

"Okay," I laughed, uncertain of how to hold it. "Clearly I have never done this before. Here it goes."

As the trimmer vibrated in my hand, I tilted my head down and made the first swipe.

"Hold on," I said, looking up into the mirror. "I didn't get anything! This is not as easy as I thought it would be. Am I holding these wrong?"

"If you angle it more this way," she replied, showing me how to hold the trimmer correctly, "you'll get more hair. Try again."

"There it goes!" I observed the buzzed section I had created. "I can't believe I'm doing it!"

"You're doing great, Nikki," Wes said, lightly grasping his hands together.

"How does it feel?" she asked me.

"A lot better now that I'm doing it right," I continued chuckling as I handed the trimmer back to her. "It was empowering, but what I ended up needing was the laughter that came with it. Thank you for allowing me to do that."

"Oh, and Wes," the hairstylist said while rubbing my shoulders. "She's ready, so you're up next to benefit from her newly discovered skill."

"I can do the first shave on his head too?" I asked, looking back toward her.

"You bet," she said. "You're a pro now!"

"That sounds great," Wes said laughing. "I'm ready for it."

After both Wes and I were finished having our heads shaved, I stared at myself in the mirror with no hair on my head. I realized that every time I had looked in the mirror over the last few years, I had avoided looking at myself and just focused on my hair. It was the first time I had intentionally looked at my face in years.

In many ways, I was broken and flawed, but when I saw myself I looked whole and beautiful. I hadn't lost a pound of weight and there was a CVC line hanging out of my chest, but I smiled genuinely at the person I saw.

> *I praise you, for I am fearfully and wonderfully made. Wonderful are your works; my soul knows it very well.* (Psalm 139:14)

It went even deeper than appearances. I finally understood that I was handcrafted by God and covered with his fingerprints. I had been ashamed of the way I looked, but I was able to look upon myself with love with the same eyes that look upon me from my Creator.

God had always seen me this way and now I was able to see myself in that way too. It felt like a miraculous answer to prayer.

Wes and I walked over to the same spot where we had taken our "before" photo. We snapped one more to record an "after" photo since we were both bald. When we went to the counter to pay for the services, they refused our payment.

"You all will absolutely not be paying for this today," our hairstylist told us as she hugged us goodbye. "This is a gift from me to you. Now go and beat this cancer, girl."

"Wow! Thank you!" I replied. "I'm certainly going to try."

We sent pictures to family and friends and everyone was incredibly encouraging. We laughed as friends gave Wes a hard time saying that I looked better bald than he did.

I continued being pushed beyond my limits only to be met with reassurance, assistance, and strength from my faith and those around me. With every challenge we had faced, we found hope.

When I lay down to sleep that night, I shivered without having my hair covering my neck. The pillowcase felt wet making direct contact with my scalp and I knew it would take a few days to adjust to it. I wrapped my body up with the down comforter on the bed and nestled up next to Wes to fall asleep. He held me tightly, warming my heart and body.

My aggressive round of chemo was scheduled for next week. I knew the side effects wouldn't stop at hair loss. Since each person responds to treatment differently, I prayed fiercely each day and tried to rest in preparation for the storm that was on its way.

As for that day, I was bald—and I felt beautiful.

14

The Calm Before the Storm

The day of my aggressive chemo treatment had arrived and Wes and I were exhausted. Fatigue had been the only side effect I had experienced so far, but it made every activity feel like a chore. Wes had been diagnosed with an ear infection and it had been incredibly painful for him. We both weren't sleeping well, and we had a long day up ahead at the cancer center.

"How's Wes doing?" my mom asked as I filled up our water bottles in the kitchen.

"He's not doing too well," I shared with her. "His ear infection has only worsened and he barely got any sleep last night. He told me this morning that he feels guilty for being sick because he wants to be there for me."

"He loves you so much," she told me. "Is he going with you to chemo today?"

"He is," I told her while grabbing our backpack to put in the car. "I told him he didn't have to come, but he said he doesn't want to miss it."

"Do you think he'll be well enough to fly to Colorado next week to move your stuff out of your house into the storage unit?"

"I hope so," I said.

Breaking the lease on our house in Colorado had been one of the hardest decisions we had to make. When we found out that I would be treated in Texas for nine months, we knew we couldn't continue paying the rent. Even with all the generous donations coming in, it just didn't make sense to keep the house. The leasing agent had already found new tenants to move into it, so we didn't have long to get our belongings moved out before they moved in.

The house in Colorado had been a blessing to us, and I would forever love all its quirky features. But "home" was anywhere I was with Wes. And right now home was located in a spare bedroom at my parents' house.

Wes and his family were going to move all our items into storage while I stayed behind in Texas since we had no idea of what type of side effects I would be experiencing.

"Guess what I am taking to the cancer center today?" I asked while reaching into the backpack. I pulled out a pair of Mickey Mouse ears that I would wear when going to the Disney parks.

"What are you doing with those?" my mom asked laughing.

"I decided that I'm going to wear my mouse ears during every chemotherapy session!" I exclaimed. "I grabbed them from our last visit to Colorado. I thought they might bring hope and joy when people are fearful and struggling. They also can serve as a fun head accessory."

"I think that's great. Plus, they're cute!"

"I just have to keep them from sliding off my head," I said while modeling them for my mom as Wes entered the kitchen.

"Are you ready, Wes?" I asked him to confirm that he was still okay to go.

"I am," he replied. "I'm going to go ahead and get the car started. I'll see you in the car."

"Oh, he looks like he's feeling pretty bad," my mom said as he exited the house. "I'm praying for you both. You all drive safe and call us when you're on the way back."

"I will," I said as I hugged her goodbye and headed out the door.

Since Wes didn't feel that great, I wanted to be quiet on the drive. I was thinking about what my cancer team had shared with me:

Your second week of each cycle will be the hardest on your body.

The side effect profile was vast and unpredictable since it was impossible to know how each individual would react to treatment. This would be yet another new voyage of discovery for us.

When we took the exit leading to the MD Anderson Cancer Center, I looked over at Wes and could see him shifting around in his seat. He kept grabbing onto his ear with one hand while his other gripped tightly to the steering wheel. He was uncomfortable and upset.

"Are you okay?" I asked him.

"I can't be sick," he replied, frustrated. "This is the most difficult week for you, we have no idea what's going to happen, and I need to be healthy enough to take care of you."

My heart was crushed as I could see how upset he was. He had fully taken on the role of caregiver and it was to the point where he had pushed aside the fact that he was a person too—a person who gets sick, a person who, like me, was a patient too.

I could relate to his feelings, though. Sometimes the feeling of being a patient was one of helplessness. He had given up a lot of things to be here with me, and in his time of need, I didn't know what to do or how to help. I was only going to become sicker.

What do I possibly have to offer to him that would be helpful?

"You've already done so much for me, Wes," I reassured him. "I will do whatever I can to be here for you too."

"It's okay, Nikki," he said trying to put on a positive face. I took out the backpack and put my Mickey Mouse ears on.

"Hey—look at that," he said while grinning. "Those do help put people in a good mood. It's working for me. Everyone's going to love them."

"If none of us here can be at a Disney park," I told him, "we'll bring Disney to them!"

When we walked into the cancer center the mouse ears brought smiles and became a great conversation starter. On the way to my chemotherapy appointment, we met a lot of people walking up and down the halls. It had been a great opportunity to see joy come alive, and it kept my mind off the treatment ahead.

This one was a little longer than the first, totaling two and a half hours of medication administration. I wasn't as nervous about the appointment since I knew what to expect from the first treatment, but it was what would happen when we finished that gave me goosebumps when I thought about it.

We arrived at the Ambulatory Treatment Center and were placed into a patient room similar to the one we were in the week before. We waited for the nurse to hook up Carl to the IV line. I went ahead and wrapped up in the same fluffy pink blanket that accompanied us during our first chemo treatment to get comfortable while we waited.

I looked over at Wes and saw that he was already falling asleep in the chair next to the bed. I looked upon him with such compassion. He had suffered through a rough night with a continual pounding in his ear, and I could tell that the conversations we had with everyone in the halls about my mouse ears had understandably worn him out.

I took off my Mickey Mouse ears and sat up quietly to place them on top of the backpack next to him, trying not to wake him. His eyes popped open as I got close and I waved at him and blew him a kiss. Without saying a word, he moved out of his chair and crawled up onto my cot-size hospital bed, and cuddled with me. He made sure that I was okay, rested his head on my chest, and fell asleep within minutes.

When the nurse came to start the chemo, she was extra quiet in an attempt not to wake him. Even with chemo running through my veins, it was such a tranquil moment for me.

As the hours went by, he rested while I had my arm wrapped around him. Feeling the warmth of his body so peaceful right beside me almost caused me to forget where we were.

Even in my fragile state, I had something to offer him. I wasn't a "caregiver," but I was able to give my husband the care he needed at that moment.

Usually, when I saw my wristband I was reminded that I was a patient. But today I provided my husband a place to rest his weary head to sleep and to heal and was reminded that I was also a wife. He slept while I smiled through the entire treatment.

When the machine beeped and time was up, Wes woke up. I was then given an injection that would help keep my immune system up and then we were released to go.

"Now this could cause some pain and discomfort later on," she said. "Let us know if you have any problems with this injection."

Cycle one was almost complete. I would have one week of rest and recovery before I began the process again. My world seemed okay for now. Manageable even.

When we arrived back at my parents' house, they were sitting in the living room with their eyes glued to the television.

"You guys need to see this," my dad said, waving us in from the front door.

"What's going on?" I asked him as we entered the living room.

"It's a hurricane," he said as he turned to me and pointed back at the screen. "It's heading right for us."

We were definitely not in Colorado anymore.

"Aren't you supposed to be flying back to Colorado to move all of your stuff into storage this week?" my mom asked Wes.

"That *is* this week!" he replied. He realized that there was no chance of this happening. "I need to make some phone calls."

I never imagined that chemo treatment would be the calmest part of my day. I guess that's what they call "the calm before the storm." Not only would unexpected side effects unfurl in the coming days, but we had no clue what was in store for us with a brooding natural disaster heading our way.

They were calling it Hurricane Harvey.

15

The Hurricane

Hurricane Harvey arrived in all its power and might, wreaking havoc all around us. I had seen natural disasters before on national news, but I had never been part of one. As I watched reporters showing videos of the hurricane on the television screen, I was watching it happen live as I looked outside my parents' windows.

Hurricane Harvey had already charged on for three days. We were on lockdown at my parents' house as the rain hadn't let up in the slightest. Even though we were an hour north of Houston, we were receiving either a flood warning or tornado alert for the area every hour.

In addition to the hurricane, things were not going well for me. I had never been in such a state of lassitude in my life. It felt as if I had cinder blocks sitting on my eye sockets and I couldn't shift my eyes without their hurting tremendously. But the worst side effect I was experiencing was uncontrollable joint pain that had been relentless over the last twenty-four hours. So much was happening all around me and inside me.

Even the MD Anderson Cancer Center was on a complete lockdown for the weekend, so no one was getting in or going out. Patients and medical staff were unable to leave the hospital because of the horrific weather and flooded streets.

"There aren't any flights leaving the area," I heard Wes whispering from across the room on the phone. "We have to be moved out this weekend—there are other tenants scheduled to move in."

Wes had finally started feeling better from his ear infection and was doing everything he could to find a way back to Colorado. He was on the phone with his parents while I was lying on the couch staring blankly ahead at The Weather Channel. Suddenly the screen went black.

"We just lost power," I heard my dad say from the other room as I noticed that all the lights had gone off too.

Wes hung up the phone and headed toward me with a forced smile.

"How are you, sweetie?" he asked me while he knelt beside the couch. "I don't want you to worry about anything. Everything is going to be fine."

"My joint pain is worsening," I disclosed to him. "I have been on the maximum dose of painkillers for twelve hours now and nothing is curving the pain. I can't move. It's taking everything within me not to cry."

"Do we need to take you to a hospital?" he inquired.

"I hope not. That seems incredibly dangerous."

When the power booted back on in the next half hour, I wanted to go to sleep. It was only 6:00 p.m. but I had barely slept at all since my joints started throbbing in pain. I lifted my fragile body up, grabbed my water bottle, and slowly walked to our bedroom. Each step was becoming more and more intolerable.

By the time I reached the bedroom, the stinging began searing throughout my entire body as if I had just walked through fire. I had reached my maximum threshold for pain. My water bottle dropped from my hand onto the floor and I doubled over the side of the bed. I couldn't hold myself up anymore and with the last ounce of energy I had left, I called out to Wes.

"Help!" I shouted out as loudly as I could. Footsteps came racing into the bedroom.

"What's going on?" Wes asked as he helped me stand up from the bed. "Are you okay?"

"The nurse said," I breathed heavily while weak in his arms, which were holding me up, "the nurse said that this could happen from the medication they injected me with after chemo to boost my immune system."

My pain was unbearable. Tears streamed down my face as fast as the rain was crashing down outside. The cancer center was closed but I knew deep down that I needed to go to an emergency room.

"I'm going to take your temperature," Wes said as he sat me down on the edge of the bed and quickly grabbed the thermometer from the other room. I took it from him and placed it under my tongue.

"It's over one hundred degrees Fahrenheit," I shared as I handed it back to him.

"We need to get you to a hospital, Nicole," he said.

"I'm driving," my dad said as he peaked his head into the bedroom, having overheard our conversation. "We're going to do the best we can to get you there."

My dad was usually a jokester, but he was dead serious about this.

While he started getting ready, Wes' phone received a text message. It was from one of his friends in Colorado asking if he could FaceTime with us.

"He is so sweet, but please tell him another time would be better," I said. "I feel terrible."

Wes sent him a text saying that it wasn't a good time for us, but he wrote back almost instantly to try and change our minds.

"He said it's important and we don't need to be on the phone for long," Wes said.

"Okay," I agreed while wiping tears from my eyes.

"My phone is ringing," Wes said as he held up his phone to show me. "It's a FaceTime call."

"Go ahead and answer it," I told him. "I don't know how long I can be on the phone, though."

To our surprise, when we answered the phone it wasn't his friend. The phone had been faced outward toward a pastor we knew in Colorado. He was praying for us and saying a blessing that sounded as if it were over a meal. It looked like he was outside. We were both really confused.

When the pastor ended his prayer, the phone was lifted up to show over one hundred fifty people gathered in a park together.

"What is this?" I asked, perplexed, looking over at Wes.

"I have no idea."

One of his coworker's wives got on the phone.

"Nicole and Wes, when we found out that you were going to Texas for treatment, we couldn't sit idly by," she shared with us. "A group of us gathered together to create a fundraiser to help with the expenses associated with your treatment."

We both exploded into tears with surprise.

They had a silent auction with a football signed by the Denver Broncos team. They were selling shirts and cakes that said "Nicole Strong" on them. Many of Wes' coworkers and their families were there, including people from the community.

"Food has been catered and there's a hairstylist who volunteered her time to shave people's heads for the event," she continued.

Over the next five minutes, people came to the phone to say hello to us and encourage us. All we could do was smile, wave, and cry. It was unreal.

We couldn't even imagine the hours this had taken and the number of people it had required to pull this event together. We were appreciative of what everyone had done to contribute to the event and support us. It was unbelievably kind and felt like a dream.

I didn't want the moment to end. It was hard to say goodbye but we needed to get me to a hospital.

For a brief moment, this big act of love distracted me from the pain I was in and provided the temporary relief I needed to stand up and get to the car.

God, your timing is perfect. I am humbled by your love and the way you continue to rescue me. Thank you for these loyal friends and loving members of the community. Thank you for caring for us and providing for us through those around us.

It was time to shift our focus on getting to the hospital. Dad opened the garage door, which loudened the violent downpour of rain. He ran outside to fire up the car and then motioned Wes and me to head that way. The wind was blowing sideways and within a few steps, we were entirely soaked.

"Are we sure this is a good idea?" I asked with the little energy I had in between breaths taken in the passenger seat.

"I'm getting you to an emergency room if it is the last thing that I do," my dad replied, kicking the car into reverse out of the driveway with eyes straining to see.

As the rain poured down, the lines couldn't be seen on the roads. The windshield wipers whipped back and forth futilely due to the near impossibility of seeing anything. It was dark and thunder roared continually over the next twenty minutes.

I bit my lip through the pain, and as we hydroplaned time and time again, I realized this drive might *be* the last thing we did. Every time we slid across the water it caused my pain to singe. I was desperate for us to arrive. We were the only vehicle on the road and as each minute passed, I wondered how we would make it out alive.

What are we doing? All three of our lives are at risk.

"Look—there it is!" my dad exclaimed.

We looked ahead and could barely see a neon sign glowing in the distance while we drifted our way into the parking lot. I couldn't believe we had made it. My dad dropped Wes and me off at the front and parked the car to meet us inside.

"Welcome," a woman said with a surprised look on her face at the check-in counter.

"Are you seeing patients?" Wes asked as he held me up next to him.

"Yes, yes, we are," she replied, scrambling to get forms together for us. "I'm just surprised to see you here. Our staff has been stuck here for three days unable to leave due to the hurricane. I'm quite astounded that you made it here."

My dad walked in and headed to the counter next to us.

"My family would have paddled a canoe to get us here if they had to," I said, leaning into Wes' arms and smiling up at my dad. They had shown great love by risking their lives to get me here.

Since I was the only patient in the waiting room, I was immediately taken back and received morphine to ease the pain.

"Wow," I said out loud with a wheeze.

"What's wrong?" Wes asked as he rushed to my side.

"The pain is gone!" I started crying tears of joy. "This is the first time I've had relief from this agonizing and excruciating pain in days. I'm so thankful. Thank you for bringing me here."

We had been there for a little over an hour when they came back with scan results they had taken when I arrived. Without any significant findings, they assumed it was a side effect from chemo or the medication that was used to boost my immune system.

"Well, believe me," I said. "I will not be taking that immune system-boosting medication again."

Wes' phone rang and he stepped out into the hall to take the call. Shortly after, they told us there wasn't anything else they could do and released us to leave.

"Well, I have some pretty great news," Wes said as he reentered the room. "I just received a phone call that the fundraiser from tonight raised $3,500 for our treatment."

"Wow!" I said in awe. "I can't believe this. How can we ever thank them?"

"We can start by writing thank you cards tomorrow if you're up for it," Wes suggested.

"I'd like that," I replied as we gathered our things and started walking toward the doors to the hospital.

"Hey—it looks like the rain has died down," my dad said as we were close enough to look outside.

"This is the first time it's let up in days," I replied in amazement with the timing of it all.

"Let's go home," my dad said as we walked out to the car together.

Dad drove cautiously through the flooded streets on our route back to my parents' house. Without the rain pouring down, it was a much smoother and safer drive than it had been on the way to the hospital.

God had sent us the help we needed. We witnessed a prayer being answered in ways unimaginable to us. My dad and my husband had put their lives on the line for me to help me get out of pain and the medical team at the hospital took great care of me. All the while, Wes' coworkers and our friends from Colorado had put on a fundraiser over one thousand miles away for us to help support us during treatment.

As cancer was wreaking havoc on my body and this hurricane on the city, I was reminded that the devastation that surrounded us would be rebuilt by people who had hearts to serve, love, and sacrifice selflessly. A natural disaster and a diagnosis had only so much power to destroy. Nothing could inhibit the repairing and rebuilding that would take place in the days ahead.

After everything that happened, hope was something I had an abundance of.

When we arrived safely at home, I wrote this verse in my journal:

> *Now to him who is able to do far more abundantly than all that we ask or think, according to the power at work within us, to him be glory in the church and in Christ Jesus throughout all generations, forever and ever. Amen.* (Ephesians 3:20–21)

Even after the morphine wore off, the pain never returned. I didn't even have to take any additional pain medication. I couldn't understand why, but it was a true example of God doing more abundantly than all I could have ever asked for or thought. I fell asleep peacefully and thankfully in awe of the greatness of our God.

16

The Great Escape

It had been a week since our visit to the emergency room, and Hurricane Harvey had finally come to an end. Unfortunately, the damage it had done would linger far into the foreseeable future with the facilities and houses it had destroyed. Airlines were still shut down and many roads remained flooded. Somehow, Meagan had found a route that was drivable from Dallas and stayed with us at my parents' house during my recovery week. The week had gone by so fast with her there.

Wes had been unable to fly to Colorado, but Lisa called and told us that they had sent a group of employees from work to our house to help my in-laws with the move. She also shared that a moving company would be coming to help move everything and that we didn't have to worry about it at all. Our family, friends, and coworkers had gone out of their way to pack, clean, and move our entire home into storage. They gave us the blessing of being able to fully focus on my treatment in Texas.

It was still dark outside when I felt Wes roll over in bed.

"Good morning, my sweet!" my ever-loving husband exclaimed.

"Good morning, honey," I replied while looking around the darkened room. "What time is it?"

"It's 4:30 a.m.," he said in a forcibly upbeat tone in his attempt to wake us up. "It's time to start your second cycle of chemo."

My follow-up appointments from the first cycle of chemo had gone well, so I was approved to move on to my second of six cycles. My team wanted me to continue on the same regimen again, which was positive news to hear. In three weeks I would be evaluated with my first CT scan since we began treatment to see if the chemo was working or not.

When we arrived at the cancer center and sat down in the waiting room, I made a sour face and gripped my shirt by my chest.

"Nik, what's the matter?" Wes asked.

"Something feels different," I replied, staring blankly ahead at the television set on mute in front of us. "My chest feels heavy today. Maybe I'm just tired."

We were both worn out. I could feel the fog from chemo worsening in my head when a familiar commercial came on the television in front of us. It was an advertisement for a Pumpkin Spice Latte from Starbucks.

"Wait—is it fall already?" I asked in disbelief. "How did it get here so fast?"

"It's hard to believe it's September," he replied, shaking his head in astonishment.

"I feel like we spent the entire summer at home and in hospitals," I said, reflecting on the last couple of months. "If I'm being transparent, I miss our adventures and even the normal outings we used to be able to do. I feel so different."

"We'll get back there one day, sweetheart," he said, looking over toward the patient's doors. "It looks like they're calling you back. Are you ready to start your second cycle of treatment?"

"I am," I replied as he wrapped his arm around my waist and walked with me to the back.

After chemo, we drove to my parents' house, cooked dinner, and spent time with my parents. They loved to play board games and card games, so we made a whole evening of it. It was a great activity to stimulate my mind, and since it was low impact and low intensity, I was able to participate.

When it started getting late, my parents decided to turn in for the night. Although it had been a long day for us too, I was still wide awake. We headed into the bathroom for our nightly routine, where Wes flushed my CVC line with saline, and then we crawled into bed.

After Wes turned the lamp off on his side, I flipped mine on.

"What are you doing?" he asked as I laid my head so close to him that our noses were touching.

"Did you ever stay up late while you were living at home with your parents, trying to remain as quiet as you could so they wouldn't catch you?" I asked, trying to ramp up some fun conversation.

"All the time," he said while he sat up. "I would be up late playing video games and my heart would be racing when I heard the door handle twist. The TV was on and I was on the floor in front of it. There was nowhere for me to hide."

"That's funny," I said as I sat up to face him cross-legged on the bed. "I used to be on the house phone with my friends all through the night in our game room. I remember one time my mom woke up for the day and she hollered, 'You haven't gone to sleep yet, have you?' and I hung up the phone, ran to my room, and dove into my bed to try to hide."

"Look at us rebels," Wes laughed. "Did you ever sneak out?"

"Actually, no, I never did," I shared. "Did you?"

"No, I didn't," he replied while his eyebrows rose. "What if we snuck out of your parents' house tonight?"

"What?" I asked while whispering, afraid my parents could hear us. "Are you serious?"

"Yeah," he said. "How fun would that be? We can't get in 'trouble' since we're adults, but I bet it would be exhilarating."

"Where would we even go?" I asked while buying into his idea a bit.

"Since we're in the suburbs, I'm pretty sure the only thing open this late is Whataburger," he snickered. "Why don't we sneak out and get ourselves a burger?"

"This is hilarious," I whispered while shaking my head. "I'm feeling that nervous excitement from when I was a teenager again."

"Come on—let's do it," he insisted. "You said you were missing adventures. What's more adventurous than married young adults sneaking out of their parents' house to get Whataburger in the middle of the night?"

"You're right, you're right," I said in agreement. "You lead the way."

We carefully opened up the closet to change back into clothes to leave the house. With every squeak and creak, we would freeze to make sure we didn't hear any activity outside our door.

We slowly rotated the door handle and tip-toed toward the garage. Wes walked in front of me to make sure the coast was clear and waved me forward to keep going. We maneuvered around my parents' dogs in hopes that they wouldn't wake up, but one of their heads popped up and looked at us.

"Shh," Wes said. "It's okay—nothing to see here."

We both smiled as we continued by. Wes took his keys and when he went to place them into his pocket, they hit the floor with a crash.

We stopped breathing as we stood there as still as mannequins.

Did they hear us? Are we about to get caught?

The minute we stood still felt like an hour, but we didn't hear any movement from my parents' room. We made our way to the front door and unlocked it carefully and quietly, cracked it open, and slipped outside.

When we arrived at the car, we opened the door cautiously and closed it just enough for it to latch. Wes started the car as we looked at each other. We winced with our clenched teeth and squinted eyes, hoping they wouldn't wake up.

He put the car in reverse without headlights on and backed out into the road. When we made it to the road, he turned on the headlights and put the car in drive. We claimed victory as ours.

"We did it!" I shouted. "That was awesome!"

"Oh, wow," Wes said, breathing heavily. "I can't believe I dropped the keys and they still didn't wake up. Let's go get a burger and celebrate!"

After picking up our burgers and exiting the drive-through, we pulled into the parking lot and faced the empty road in front of us.

A fast-food burger had never tasted so sweet, having been birthed from our spontaneous jaunt.

I didn't know what would become of me as my body was weakening and we were unsure if treatment was even working. Wes was doing everything in his power to make every moment we had together count. It didn't matter that summer had come and gone because we had each other now.

When we drove back to my parents' house, we turned off the headlights while pulling back into the driveway. We expected them to be sitting on the couch with a single lamp turned on while in their robes, as in the movies, but it was just as silent as when we had left. We had successfully snuck in and out without waking them up.

After brushing our teeth, changing back into our pajamas, and crawling back into bed, it felt as if we could do anything. It had been fun, life-giving, and exciting. I loved the memory we had created together.

We ended the night with a high five and a kiss.

17

Surprise

More side effects developed over the last week. My medical team had told me that as more chemo entered my body I would likely experience increased side effects and that current ones could intensify.

An interesting one that arose was a loss of taste. I could feel the textures of things that I would chew, but everything I consumed produced no flavor from my taste buds. One of the last things I had been able to taste was the burger on our late-night Whataburger escape.

We had been pleasantly overwhelmed by all the uplifting phone calls and text messages that were continuing to come from Colorado and from friends in Texas. Donations, cards, letters, and care packages arrived every week since we had relocated to Houston.

I found great joy in writing letters and sending cards to people. We made it a priority to write a thank you card for every gift we received too. It made us feel that we could express our love to those far away from us during treatment.

Wes and I had spent the majority of the day at the MD Anderson Cancer Center for the intense week two combination of chemo to be administered. I dozed off during most of it while Wes read and we were overjoyed to hear the machine beep, signaling the conclusion of treatment for the day.

"All right," my nurse said to me as she approached me to disconnect my CVC line from the IV. "Let me get you set up with the immune system-boosting injection."

"I spoke with Dr. Conley and he said I could opt out of taking it since the pain from it sent me to the emergency room last time," I replied, shuddering from my recent experience with it.

"Okay," she responded. "There's a high risk that your blood cell counts will lower. They will follow up with you on blood work to monitor you closely."

I don't know if I'll regret this or not, but it has to be better than going back to the emergency room. Right?

After we were cleared to leave without having the injection, we began the drive back up north to my parents' house. All of us decided to watch a movie together on the couches since it had been a long day for everyone. The dogs were snuggled up at our feet and it was exactly what we all had needed.

About halfway through the movie, I reclined and reached my arms over my head for a stretch. As I lengthened my body, I felt resistance in my right arm, causing me to flinch and bring it back to my chest.

"Wes, do you remember if I had heaviness in my arm the last cycle?" I whispered while trying not to disrupt the movie.

"No," he replied, leaning up to take a look at it. "I think you just shared that you had heaviness in your chest. Maybe try to sleep with your arm above your head tonight to help with blood flow."

"That's a good idea," I said. "I'll try that."

I was slightly concerned but it was hard to know what was normal and what was severe. When we finished the movie and got ready for bed, we decided we would reassess how it was doing in the morning and decide the next steps from there.

The morning came quickly, and I rolled over toward Wes to say good morning.

"Whoa!" I exclaimed. My arm hurt with the weight of my body on top of it.

"What's the matter?" Wes asked as he rolled over in bed toward me.

"My right arm," I replied while jolting my body up to seated. I held my right arm up with my left and moved it closer to my face. It was incredibly swollen and a light shade of red.

"We need to call Dr. Conley right away," Wes said as he rubbed his eyes and jumped out of bed. He went to grab his phone to make the call.

I was completely exhausted. From an entire day at the cancer center yesterday to the side effects I was experiencing today, heading back to Houston was the last place I wanted to go. This could be serious, though, so I had to find the strength if we needed to go.

"It's time to get dressed," Wes said as he poked his head back into the room. "They're going to work you in to be seen this morning. We need to leave as soon as possible."

We arrived at the cancer center about an hour later. As soon as we walked into the Sarcoma Center, I could see my nurse out in the waiting room. It was the fastest that I had been seen and I was immediately sent to have an ultrasound of my arm completed.

"Mrs. Body?" I heard my name being called by the doorway to have the test done.

I turned around and shook my head as Wes nodded his and blew me a kiss. I had no idea what was going on, but it had seemed urgent enough for this to be happening within the same day.

The test went by quickly. In the past, it was the longer examinations that worried me, so I wondered if maybe nothing was wrong and that this was a normal side effect.

"If you'll wait here, we'll have a radiologist look at the images now and let you know if he finds anything," the ultrasound tech instructed. "He'll give you a call here in the next ten minutes or so."

This was a first for me as I sat in the imaging room alone while waiting for a phone call. I had become quite accustomed to waiting for results over the last few months, so I tried not to let my mind wander, knowing the destructive path it could lead me down.

I heard my phone vibrating on the counter where I had placed it during the test, so I stood up to pick it up and answer.

"Mrs. Body?" I heard a gentleman on the other end of the phone say.

"This is she," I replied, sitting down at the edge of the patient bed. My heart started beating fast.

"Hi—I'm calling with the results of your ultrasound," he said. "We found something."

I gripped the edge of the bed as if to brace for impact.

"There's a blood clot in your right jugular vein," he said, enunciating each word.

I swallowed the lump that had formed in my throat and exhaled loudly.

"What would have caused this?" I asked, trying to understand. "Is it because I didn't take the injection for my immune system?"

"No, it has nothing to do with that. Blood clots can occur in patients who have a CVC line. The vein detects a foreign object, which is the catheter, and tries to fight back by clotting."

Thanks, Carl.

"I guess that makes sense," I said, gaining a better understanding of why this was happening.

"We're going to need to get you on a blood thinner," he instructed. "You have an appointment in an hour with your oncologist to get you set up with that. You can start heading that way now if you'd like."

"Thank you." We said our goodbyes and ended the call.

When I shared the news with Wes, I could see a concerned look across his face that I had never seen before.

"The right jugular vein is very close in proximity to the brain," he said as we walked back to the Sarcoma Center for further guidance. "I'm very glad we came in today to have this looked at."

After I was prescribed a blood thinner, we headed back to my parents' house.

It was possible I wouldn't live through this. If the blood clot moved, it could kill me.

For the first time, it hit me that I may not see the other end of cancer-free on earth.

My heart broke when we told friends and family about the news. The heaviness in their voices and the mortified looks in their eyes were unable to be hidden. The blood clot had pushed everyone over the edge.

In our complete exhaustion, we sat down in the living room together.

"We'll do this together," Wes said while we sat on the couch. "Let's put all of our focus on what we can do. You'll take your medication every day and we'll continue on your treatment plan."

He was right. I couldn't lose the fight within me now. We had taken on many obstacles like this already, and I didn't want to allow myself to lose hope. Even though we didn't have control of a lot of what was happening in my body, we could continue following the treatment plan, ask questions, get plenty of rest, and speak up if we had concerns.

In some areas, we felt as though cancer had paralyzed us. In other ways, we were finding our voices and leaning into God more than we ever had before. It had been exceedingly challenging, but we were more determined than ever.

As we wrapped up the evening, we decided to pray the words of the

Serenity Prayer to soothe us to sleep:

> *God, grant me the serenity to accept the things I cannot change, courage to change the things I can, and wisdom to know the difference.*

18

The Concert

It had been three days since my aggressive round of chemo, and I hadn't spoken a word.

In addition to the emergence of the blood clot, mouth sores started lining my inner cheeks, making it hard for me to talk and eat. Thrush caused a relentless throbbing in my mouth while also turning my cheeks and tongue gray. And my head was now completely smooth as chemo had finally taken my hair completely.

My daily medicinal intake had increased even more. I had opted out of the immune system-boosting medication that had sent me to the emergency room after the last cycle, but that meant that I was now highly susceptible to getting sick if I left the house. I spent my days lying in bed and walking around the house with clenched teeth to try alleviating the pain.

As I lay in bed, the comforter was pulled up to my neck. I was motionless except for the movement that occurred with breathing. I looked up at the ceiling fan and caught hold of one of the blades and watched as it circled around and around. I didn't know the time, nor did I care. I didn't want to move.

How long would this last?

Wes had done everything he could to bring a smile to my face. He would show me funny pictures and videos, read to me, tell me jokes, rub my back, and kiss my forehead. I would try to smile and nod to let him know that I loved him, but I had a heaviness in my body and my heart that withheld me from joyfully responding.

I was in agony.

I slowly rolled my aching body out of bed and walked toward the door where my robe was hanging up. I placed it upon my fatigued body and quietly headed to the bathroom to draw a bath. I had been taking four baths each day because they seemed like the only place I could find comfort and relief.

When I submerged into the hot water, I took a deep breath in through my nose and felt the clench of my jaw release upon exhale. I hunched over and stared blankly ahead as the water moved around me to the sound of a humming faucet. The room began blurring.

It won't be like this forever. I will find my way back to joy and healing.

The bathroom door creaked open. It scared me and I swung my head to the right to see Wes enter with a huge grin on his face. He continued through the door while whistling and looking around the room as if he had a plan in mind.

I couldn't help but shake my head and reveal a half-smile. After three days, he still exuded energy in his hopeful heart that he could find a way to help me through this.

I looked at him with playful eyes and a suspicious smirk while I turned off the water to see what he was up to. But surprisingly, he didn't say a word. He sat down opposite me next to the bathtub facing my direction and started fiddling on his phone. I couldn't figure out what he was doing because he wasn't looking at me.

Maybe he thought that his presence would be the comfort I needed. It's really nice.

After minutes of silence, I started feeling chilled and dipped my hands into the water to fill up my palms and pour it down my arms. I was interrupted when music began to play from his phone, causing me to look back up to him. He played an old song by The Del-Vikings.

He began singing to me and tapped his toes while I watched him attentively. He was bobbing his head with expanded eyes as if to invite me to sing with him. I smiled and shook my head no.

"I guess this one isn't working," he said without feeling defeated. "How about we try another one?"

In addition to tapping his toes to an upbeat song by Little Richard, he grabbed the bottle of body wash sitting on the edge of the bathtub and put it up to his mouth to use as a microphone. Before I knew it, he was singing loudly.

I couldn't help but beam joy. He was adorable and animated. He could see my eyes light up, so he changed the song again to keep up the energy.

He started dancing and singing to a sweet love song that played. With every lyric he sang, I felt walls coming down around my heart and soul. The joy that was abounding in my core started overpowering the pain that I had been enduring. I started wiggling my toes against the edge of the bathtub to the beat to let him know I was sold on his performance.

Wes looked over and saw that I was participating and his smile widened. He leaned over the bathtub and extended his arm toward me with the bottle of body wash in his hand. He wiggled the bottle slightly and his eyes pleaded for me to sing along. He was passing the "microphone" and I had a decision to make.

I paused the tapping of my toes and could feel the pain that radiated from my body. A spark fanned into flame within me and I grinned while removing the bottle from his hand claiming my role as the new lead singer. Before I knew it, I was on my feet in the bathtub while water splashed everywhere as I put on a concert for Wes.

The pain seared, but I was singing, dancing, pointing at him, and laughing as I declared my love for him through song. He was clapping along and cheering as he looked up at me. He had broken seventy-two hours of silence.

"I can't help myself," I sang from the top of my lungs. "I love you and nobody else!"

The last words trailed off as I began losing my breath.

"Oh, Wes." I covered my mouth while the bottle of body wash fell from my hand and splashed in the bathtub. "I *do* love you. Thank you for not giving up on me. I have felt so broken and so lost."

Tears of joy trickled down my face as I lowered myself to my knees. I hugged Wes tightly over the edge of the bathtub. Water covered the walls, tile floor, and his shirt, but I never wanted to let him go.

It had been the longest three days of my life. When I assessed my pain at that moment, I realized it had been bad but not debilitating to the point at which I couldn't talk and function. Something more had been going on with me:

I realized I had been depressed.

It caught me off guard because I had always tried to find the positives in life. What I had been unknowingly doing was suppressing my feelings all this week. It must have gotten so great that it had manifested as depression within and had welled up to the surface.

Even though my mouth was aching, I shared my heart with Wes to bring awareness to us both about what I had been going through. By keeping the line of communication open, we would be able to talk through it or get me help if we noticed it happening again. He encouraged me to continue expressing my feelings and sharing my thoughts with him. I couldn't believe it took a concert in the bathtub to uncover something so deep.

"I love you, Nicole," he whispered. "I will never give up on you."

"I love you too," I replied quietly. I knew that even though the night would be hard, I could make it through.

"At the end of next week we finally get to see how well the treatment is working," he reminded me while handing me a towel to dry off with.

Has all this been worth it? Would this struggle and suffering result in a shrinking tumor? Or has the cancer been growing and spreading all over my body?

I was nervous yet hopeful. As I glanced back at Wes, I could see my love was expanding for him beyond what I thought was humanly possible. I toweled off and got dressed and we snuggled up next to each other in bed.

One week to go.

19

A New Word

I felt much better than I did a few days ago, demonstrating that the recovery week had fulfilled its purpose. Wes and I packed a bag and made our way to the cancer center for the evaluation of the first two cycles of chemo. It was our first checkpoint since I had begun treatment and would answer the question we had been asking since chemo began:

Is this working?

I laughed when I found out that the scan they would perform was the same as the one from months ago that made me feel as if I had wet my pants. After having that CT scan in Colorado, I never thought I would have to do that again. However, I found myself back in the all-familiar room stretched out with an IV in my arm following the breathing instructions from the electronic voice from the machine.

Having an extra set of clothes in my backpack made me feel secure, but I was relieved to discover that I had made it through the scan just fine without having an "accident." All we needed to do now was wait for the results.

When we arrived at the waiting room at the Sarcoma Center, it was quite full of patients. Almost every seat had been taken, but we found two next to each other and sat down. There was still about an hour until my appointment, so I decided to strike up a conversation with the lady next to me to keep my mind off things.

I learned that she had flown in from South Carolina and would come here every couple of months to be scanned after she had chemo administered back home. She had come alone while her husband watched her children back in South Carolina. She was in the same boat as me, waiting for results.

"Are you having *scanxiety*?" she asked me after we had talked for a while.

"Scanxiety?" I repeated the unfamiliar term. "I'm not quite sure I know what that is."

"You haven't heard of that?" she asked me, sounding slightly surprised. "It's a term that a lot of cancer patients use to explain the anxiety they get associated with waiting for results from their scans."

"That's clever," I laughed. "I would have to say that sums up how I feel right now. It helps to stay busy talking to someone while I wait."

"I've been coming here for over a year now, and I still get scanxiety," she confessed.

"I completely understand that," I said, feeling a stirring in my heart. "Can I pray with you?"

"Yes, you can," she replied as she instantly took my hand as though we had known each other for years.

We sat together with our heads bowed and prayed for our families, our results, and our anxious hearts. We had become unlikely friends connected by cancer and we sought out peace with each other to God. When she was called back we hugged, saying that we hoped we would see each other again someday.

As the minutes ticked by, the waiting room started emptying and patients were being taken back to be seen one by one. Anytime I saw Leslie come up to the front my heart skipped a beat, but it wasn't my time to go back yet. As I sat next to Wes, my mind started wandering.

What if this isn't working? What would be the next steps? Can my body even endure more cycles?

My palms were sweating, and I folded my hands over each other repeatedly. My foot began tapping while my breathing was getting heavier. Scanxiety, as the patient referred to it, was starting to take root within me.

Although I had learned a new term, this hadn't been an unfamiliar place for me to be in. With the little energy I had gained back, I didn't want to spend it on worrying.

I took a moment to ask myself a question to combat my scanxiety:

When was the last time that worrying helped me?

I couldn't recall a single time when it had. If anything, it had caused grief, destruction, and unhealthy daydreams in my mind. It made me think about a verse that I had heard often on anxiety and worrying:

> *Which of you by being anxious can add a single hour to his span of life?* (Matthew 6:27)

The answer was obvious but I needed to ask myself that question. These were words I knew and remembered, but it was so difficult to put them into practice. I wanted to overcome this by focusing on what I could control.

"Nicole Body," we heard Leslie say across the waiting room.

My time had finally arrived. We stood up and walked toward her and she took us back to a patient room. It wouldn't be long until we received the results from my scan.

"I can't imagine how difficult Dr. Conley's job must be," I told Wes as we sat and waited. "Each room that he goes into has a patient on the edge of his or her seat wishing, hoping, and praying that the words he says will contain good news. Can you imagine how hard it would be to deliver bad news in that situation?"

"It takes a special person to do what he does," he said in agreement. "I love that he fights for the underdog by specializing in this rare and aggressive cancer."

"I hope the results are good," I told Wes honestly.

"Me too. No matter what the results say, we'll find the best treatment plan for you and do everything we can to keep you alive. I promise."

"Thank you," I told him. "That makes me feel a lot better. Even if the results aren't good, we'll find another way to fight this."

I heard steps growing louder and realized that they were nearing our door. I fixated my eyes on the silver handle as I watched it turn and slowly open with a familiar face peeking through.

"Nicole, it's good to see you again," Dr. Conley said as I extended my hand to shake his.

"It's good to see you too," I said breathlessly. "I have to be honest—I wasn't nervous about the results until this moment."

He sat down and lowered his head toward his notes. It felt like an eternity as I waited for him to speak his next words. He shifted his eyes back up toward me. My heart was beating fast and my eyes were laser-focused toward his.

This is it. Here it comes.

"Your tumor is shrinking, Nicole," he said with a smile. "The chemotherapy is working."

Tears came bursting forth from my eyes like a mighty waterfall. The anticipation of the results, the gratitude of the support and prayer we had received, and all the pain and unknowns we had endured came spilling out of my eyes in the form of tears.

Libby always told me that God created tears for moments where words couldn't capture the intensity of emotions. After that moment I knew it to be true.

"That's great," I choked out the words between my tears while Wes came alongside me wrapping his arms around me. "It's so great to hear this news."

"The size of your tumor has shrunk about half the size as it was before," he continued saying in an upbeat voice. "We're making progress. I would like to stay the course we're on and see what administering more chemo can do for you. How do you feel about that?"

"I think that's a great idea," I confidently replied with relief.

Before Dr. Conley exited the patient room, he explained that I would go through two more cycles before we would meet again to see if treatment was continuing to work. After a little causerie, we said our goodbyes and started leaving the cancer center.

It had been a long road thus far, but things were looking up. Even through unpredictable side effects, unexpected trials, and a blood clot, it had all been worth it for the results we received that day. All the pain and struggle had resulted in progress, which gave me an extra boost of motivation for the next cycle.

I had no idea of what to expect with cycle three around the corner. With countless uncertainties and immense physical weakness that would only increase, I knew I didn't want to be taken captive by anxiety. By spending my days weighing myself down with a million hypotheticals, I would completely wear myself out.

"Hey, Nik," Wes said to me when we sat down for dinner that night. "Your birthday falls at the end of your recovery week during this cycle."

"I can't believe it's that close," I replied in shock that it had gotten here so fast.

"We'll make it special and fun. I've already got a couple of ideas."

It was just the motivation I needed to push through the next couple of weeks.

20

The Robotic Arm

"Happy birthday, Nicole!" Wes exclaimed while waking me up. I smiled as he bent down to kiss me. I couldn't tell if he was more excited or if I was.

"We've got to get going," he said, already completely dressed and ready to go. "You have your routine end-of-cycle blood work and then I'm taking you to NASA today!"

"That sounds amazing," I said rubbing my eyes trying to wake up. "Not the blood work part, but NASA!"

I couldn't believe we had already finished cycle three. I was officially halfway through chemo treatment. It had been a grueling couple of weeks, but the burden we felt was lightened when Libby and her husband, Randy, drove down from Colorado to visit us for a few days. Each time we would get together with them, they lavished us with love, encouragement, laughter, and wisdom. Their leadership in faith and prayer helped strengthen us on the toughest days. It was exactly what we needed.

Donations, care packages, and cards overflowed out of my parents' mailbox too. All in the last week we had received a beautiful purple blanket that friends patched together for my chemo sessions, a yellow shirt that read "Fighting Sarcoma like a Princess" with the Disney castle on it made for a fundraiser, and a unicorn backpack filled with all my favorite things. Because of the generosity of others, we were also financially stable and could pay my medical bills.

After we left the cancer center from having blood work taken, I had officially completed sixty-seven total appointments at the MD Anderson Cancer Center. I could hardly believe how much God had brought us through already and I was grateful to be able to spend the rest of the day celebrating my birthday with Wes.

We were finally able to head south to the NASA Johnson Space Center in Houston. When we rounded the corner to park, we saw a giant rocket and airplane at the entrance. We couldn't wait to get inside.

The building was large and the ceilings were incredibly high. We were astonished walking in for the first time. It was filled with displays of amazing missions to space conducted by NASA and we could see the evolution of space suits for astronauts. There was even a display where we could touch a fragment from Mars. We made our way to the gift shop to see all the fun items that they had for purchasing while we waited for our tour to begin.

"Since we don't have birthday cake right now," Wes said, "why don't we try one of these freeze-dried ice cream sandwiches for space in the gift shop?"

"That sounds like fun," I said as we picked one up and took it to the counter to pay for it.

We opened the silver bag and observed the Styrofoam appearance of the sandwich. Wes shrugged his shoulders and broke it in half, giving each of us a portion to try.

"Here goes nothing," he said as we both sunk our teeth into the shockingly crunchy ice cream sandwich.

"I know my taste goes in and out during chemo," I said to him, "but does this ice cream sandwich taste nasty?"

"Indeed it does," he said with a face of disgust and we laughed together.

"Don't sign me up for space travel," I joked.

When it was time for our tour, we headed outside for the tram ride. We were able to see the actual mission control room that was used in the 1960s where the famous saying "Houston, we have a problem" came from. There had been forty-one completed missions from that room. I could hardly believe that had been done without the use of modern-day computers.

Beyond that room, on the tour, I was most intrigued by the robotics area where they created all the machinery, equipment, modes of transportation, and robots used in space. But nothing was more impressive than the final stop of the tour, where they took us to see the actual Saturn V rocket that went to the moon in 1969. It was probably bigger than a football field, and it took our breaths away.

"Aren't the advances in technology just amazing?" I said to Wes as we headed back inside the main building. "The fact that we can put a man on the moon, build cars that will drive on the moon, and can touch a fragment from Mars on earth today—it's incredible."

"Technology has become so advanced. I can't wait to see what they come up with next."

We walked toward the food court to see if we could find something to snack on. Before we made it there, our attention was captured by a freestanding machine with a robotic arm swiveling around. It was white and pink and encased in glass with a digital screen behind it, making it look futuristic. It moved around like a human arm and served yogurt with toppings based on your selections.

"What's that?" Wes asked as we drew closer to it.

"Oh, I think we found the next best thing," I said as we stood there mesmerized by this moving claw. "That robotic arm is serving frozen yogurt. That's the coolest thing I've seen all day!"

"Really?" Wes asked me surprisedly. "We just saw a *rocket.*"

"*Coolest,*" I said, making quotations around my head. "Get it?"

"You're funny," he said while reaching into his pocket to get his wallet. "We have to get one."

"How fun will it be to tell everyone we got served frozen yogurt by a robotic arm at NASA?" I said as he inserted money into the machine. "Let's do this!"

There was an option to select one flavor of frozen yogurt and two toppings. Wes made his selections and I got out my phone to take a video of this momentous occasion. We watched as the machine activated and the robotic arm grabbed a cup and put it under the spout. It dispensed frozen yogurt, filling the cup up halfway.

"This is neat," I said, still videoing the action.

It moved over to Wes' first topping, but when the toppings came out, they fell off to the sides, missing the cup almost entirely. We could tell something was malfunctioning when it came back for a second dollop of frozen yogurt.

"Wes, are you seeing this?" I started laughing.

The robotic arm started spinning the cup but it was off-center so it was getting everywhere except for inside the cup!

"Uh-oh," Wes said, pointing at the cup. We howled with laughter.

The machine slopped the last topping on before placing it in the door for Wes to retrieve. As soon as he picked it up, frozen yogurt dripped from the sides, covering his hand and falling onto the floor. I was thrilled to have it recorded so we could watch it again and again.

"I can't remember the last time I laughed that hard," I told Wes while cackling uncontrollably. "That was the best birthday present ever."

The good laugh had been great for my soul.

I was exhausted since I hadn't walked around that much since I started treatment. We went to the food court to sit down so Wes and I could share what little amount of frozen yogurt had made it into the cup.

We decided to watch the video again from my phone when suddenly it stopped due to a call that was coming in. I recognized that the number was from the cancer center.

"Hello—this is Nicole," I said, covering my other ear and heading to a quiet corner.

"Mrs. Body, I just spoke with your oncologist about your blood work from this morning."

"Is everything okay?" I asked with concern. This had been the first time receiving a call back in which they mentioned speaking with Dr. Conley.

"The numbers for your liver levels are double what they should be," she replied. "This is nothing that you did, but it can happen during treatment as a side effect, unfortunately."

"What does this mean?" I asked her.

"Dr. Conley wants you to take another recovery week with no treatment," she said. "He wants you to have more time for your body to recover and hopefully these numbers will go back to a normal level. In one week we can do blood work again to see how you're doing and make decisions about moving forward at that time."

"Thank you for letting me know," I told her as we ended the call. I headed over to Wes to share the news with him.

"That was unexpected," Wes said. "How are you feeling about the news?"

"I think I realized that even though it's hard to have a chemo treatment, I'm anxious to complete it," I replied. "I'm excited for more time for my body to recover and at the same time bummed that I have to wait."

Treatment had carried on normally through the first three cycles, and I had taken for granted that things like this could happen. The way that chemo was, I truly couldn't plan for it. It reminded me of a verse I had read before:

Many are the plans in the mind of a man, but it is the purpose of the Lord that will stand. (Proverbs 19:21)

I couldn't hang on too tightly to the plan that we had set before us. What I needed to hang on tightly to was the Lord. Things were continually changing, but his love and plan for my life would always remain the same.

When we arrived at my parents' house, we shared the news and the funny moments from the day. It had been a beautiful, interesting, fascinating, and fun birthday. Just as my focus had been at the beginning of the day, I was grateful to be able to celebrate another year of life.

After crawling into bed, I tossed and turned with restless legs. When Wes had fallen asleep, I heard my stomach growl so I quietly got out of bed to see if I could grab a quick snack. I searched in the pantry and the refrigerator, but nothing looked good. When I opened the freezer, however, I saw something quite beautiful: a real ice cream sandwich, one that was created not for space travel but for people on earth.

"Yes, this is much better," I said out loud to myself as I enjoyed my treat in the kitchen in the middle of the night.

I had no idea if I would have permanent liver damage or how long my liver levels would take to lower. I felt as if I were going to stumble through this period of waiting as the robotic arm at NASA did serving the frozen yogurt. It might be a little messy, but I was going to get there.

I brushed my teeth and headed back to bed, where I snuggled up closely to Wes. The only thing better than touching a fragment from Mars today was lying next to him that night.

21

Highs and Lows

After finishing the second week of recovery, we were waiting by the phone for the call letting us know if I could begin cycle four next week. I was hoping the numbers would look good since this was the best I had felt since starting treatment.

The phone rang and I placed it on speakerphone so Wes and my parents could listen too.

"Hello—this is Nicole," I said while holding the phone in my palm.

"Hi, Nicole," the nurse on the phone said. "I'm sorry, but your liver levels are still too high. I know this is hard news to hear, but the team wants you to take one more week off from chemo so the levels have more time to come down."

"I understand," I said to her as everyone's heads began drooping.

"We'll plan on having blood work done in a week," she said in the kindest voice. "You're doing great. Let your body rest and we'll try again next week."

"That sounds good," I told her in the most upbeat voice I could muster. "Thank you for the call."

"I'm sorry, Nicole," my mom said as I ended the call.

"It's okay," I replied to her.

"You can always hire Dr. Knife to move forward with the surgery and just be done with it all!" my dad shouted as I was walking away.

"Who's that?" I asked as I turned around to look at him, confused.

"Dr. Rusty Knife," he said as he took both thumbs and pointed them toward himself. "You know—he's the best surgeon in town."

My dad had created a funny persona about a fake surgeon who performed surgeries using a rusty knife. I was not surprised by his ridiculous hilarity in the least.

"Let me think about that," I said as I smiled a little shaking my head. "Not today. Not ever!"

"What?" He exaggerated in a high-pitched voice, acting as if he were surprised that I had turned him down. He's great at lightening the mood, but he's definitely not a surgeon.

I walked out of the kitchen and around the corner into our bedroom. I realized just how attached I was to things operating on a schedule. Even in the chaos of chemo, I felt comforted when my appointments were consistent. I was constantly being pushed out of my comfort zone and pressed into growth in developing patience, contentment, and trust in God with my life.

Now we just had to figure out what to do this week while we waited.

"Knock, knock," Wes said out loud while thumping on the door to the bedroom. "Do you mind if I come in?"

"As long as Dr. Knife isn't taking me into surgery," I laughed.

"No, it's just me," he said chuckling to himself. "Talk to me, love. How are you?"

"I'm okay," I said as I looked at the pictures we had set up on the dresser. I ran my fingers across the moments captured in time back in Colorado with Wes' family and our friends—the days when I wasn't sick. "Truthfully, I just want to go home."

"Okay, baby," Wes said while walking closer to look at the pictures with me. "Let's go home for a few days."

"Really?" I asked as I pulled back and gazed up into his eyes with mine.

"Yes, really," he said. "I still have flight credit from when I was supposed to go back to help move out of our house during the hurricane. I'll call the cancer center and make sure it's okay for us to do this, and then we can check flights."

"This is perfect," I said, feeling the light come back into my eyes. "I'm so excited!"

"Maybe we can even leave tomorrow," he said while inputting the phone number to dial. "We have a week off and this is the best you've felt in a while. It would be perfect."

After Wes made the phone call to the cancer center, in which they approved our travel back to Colorado, we booked a flight for the following day and packed our bags.

"I'm going to call my folks and let them know," he said, grabbing his phone to call them.

"No, wait," I said, holding out my hand. "What if we surprise them and just show up?"

"Oh, yes," he said as he put his phone back into his pocket. "This is perfect! They're going to be so surprised!"

"Call and tell them we have a 'package' that will be arriving tomorrow evening for your mom's birthday since it's in a few days," I plotted with him. "What they *won't* know is that the 'package' is *us*!"

"We might have to catch my mom from fainting when she sees us at the door," he said to me, laughing along.

"Hopefully this will be an amazing birthday surprise for her," I told him while we strategized how we were going to pull it off.

It was great to mostly feel like myself again and to have enough energy to do something spontaneous and sweet for someone else.

I didn't sleep a wink that night due to the excitement. The flight to Colorado went smoothly and we rented a car after we landed to start driving to Wes' parents' house from the Denver airport.

"Do you think they have any idea we're coming?" I asked Wes.

"I called Dad at the airport, and he doesn't have a clue," Wes laughed. "He's concerned that the package won't arrive today since it's almost 8:00 p.m. This is going to be epic."

Even though it was mostly dark outside, we parked about four houses down to make sure we weren't seen. We quietly climbed out of the vehicle.

"All right, now—remember the plan," I said, starting to recap. "When we're one house away, let's make the call asking them to check the front door one more time for the package, okay?"

"Got it," he said as he gently closed the car door.

He started walking toward the curb, and I grabbed my purse from the backseat. After I closed the door, I looked up and saw that Wes was already on the phone making the call.

"Wes," I whispered. "You were supposed to wait before you called! We're still four houses away!"

"I'm so sorry," he mouthed at me and we both began silently laughing. "This is just so exciting. We have to run!"

We took off running toward their house in hopes that the surprise would still work.

Just as we got up the driveway, we saw the garage door open and Wes' dad walking outside on the phone. He made eye contact with Wes while holding the phone up to his ear, but it hadn't registered yet that he was looking at his son. He squinted as if trying to see him better through the dusk.

When his brain caught up with his eyes, he shouted exuberantly and wrapped Wes and me up in the biggest hug.

"Does your mother know?" he asked Wes as he pulled back, wiping tears from his eyes.

"No, she doesn't." Wes smiled, excited to surprise his mom as well.

"Perfect," his dad replied. "This is going to be fun to watch. I'll shout to her upstairs and ask her to get the door after you ring it."

We rang the doorbell a couple of times so she knew that Bode wasn't answering it. We heard the footsteps coming toward the door. Kathy opened the door and looked through the screen at both of us.

At first, she displayed a blank stare. We were smiling ear to ear as we saw her tilt her head with a questioning look. Then just as Bode had done, it clicked that she was looking at us.

"It's you!" she screamed and started bawling as she swung the door open. "It's you! It's you! It's really you!"

Kathy came straight to me. She held me close while she sobbed. Her whole body was shaking. She loved us more than her body could even contain. I had missed her more than words could have captured and I cried along with her.

We stood in one another's embrace for minutes in the doorway. I knew I would take this hug back with me to Houston for the hardest days. It was exactly what I needed and I think it was what she needed too.

"You get in for a hug too," she said to Wes, crying while she held him tightly.

"Come inside. Come inside," Bode said, waving us indoors. Their Scottish Terrier barked and twirled in circles, echoing the excitement.

"You can add this to your list of stories now," I told her. "Like the story you told us at the barbeque about you and Bode with the spider in your room. I can't wait to relive this one over and over again."

"Oh, you bet!" she replied excitedly.

She began brewing us some decaf coffee in the kitchen while the rest of us walked into the living room.

"Hey, I recognize that recliner chair," I said since it was the one they had let us borrow while I recovered post-surgery in July.

"It's all yours," Kathy said.

The recliner was a dual reminder to me about how much my family loved me and that I could recover from surgery with time. I knew I would have to be in a recliner again after the Whipple procedure. Although it would be hard, seeing the recliner reminded me that I could do it.

We spent the night reliving the surprise over and over, which brought lots of tears and laughter. Each time it was told was more beautiful than the last.

The next few days proved to be even more unforgettable. They were filled with family and friends having rich conversations and making time for prayer. We decided to have Thanksgiving with Wes' family even though it was just a few days before Halloween. It was the perfect combination of family, turkey, and candy.

When the day arrived for us to go back to Texas, my soul felt full. Since we knew we wouldn't be back for a while, we said heartfelt goodbyes and headed back to the airport.

It was worth the delay in treatment. An unexpected twist had turned into a beautiful blessing. Wes slept during most of the flight home, so I spent a lot of time in prayer on the plane.

I'm thankful that in the many surprises of this life, during the incredible highs and most devastating lows, that you, God, are constant. When we're surprised, I'm comforted by the fact that nothing is a surprise to you. You are in control and you are good. Thank you for guiding me through the challenging surprises I face and for bringing joy through beautiful ones. Please prepare my heart for whatever surprises are up ahead.

When we arrived back in Texas, I realized that blood work was scheduled for tomorrow morning. All I could think about was—

What surprises will that bring?

22

Dating You

It took three recovery weeks, but my blood work finally came back down to a level that was safe for me to continue chemo into cycle four. My medical team was concerned that my body wouldn't be able to handle it at the current dose I had been taking, so they lowered it to see if I would be able to tolerate it that way.

Concerns were raised that treatment might not prove effective with a lower dose of chemo, though. Without having the full potency of the medication in my body, there was a chance that it would not be strong enough to shrink the tumor. In addition to that, it was impossible to know if we had taken steps backward with the delay of treatment.

There was only one way to move now: *forward.*

I was well into the first week of cycle four, with chemo administered earlier in the week on Halloween. We found ourselves in the early days of November. The Houston Astros won the World Series that week. It was nice for the city to experience a victory while recovering from the horrendous hurricane that had struck a couple of months before.

Unsurprisingly, it wasn't long until I felt the medication knock me down again. What did surprise me was how the soreness, muscle aches, tender skin, fatigue, and vertigo plagued me even at a lower dose of chemo. I spent most of the week asleep in bed. If Wes didn't come into the room to bring my medication to me, I would sleep all day.

I heard Wes walk through the door.

"Hey, you," he whispered quietly to me as he entered the dark room. "Why don't you come out into the living room with me?"

"Oh, I'm not sure," I replied in my weakness. "I can barely move."

"Your parents went out to dinner," he said. "It's just me."

I couldn't believe it was already evening. I hadn't gotten out of bed all day.

I slowly got up and followed him into the living room.

He centered us in the living room between the couches while the dogs gathered around us like an audience waiting for a performance. I stood there with my eyes half-opened watching as he reached for his phone. A melody began playing and he leaned over to set the phone on the couch. He wrapped me up in his arms and began dancing with me. I didn't recognize the song, but I could tell he knew it from the way he was swaying us to the rhythm.

I smiled through the fog in my head and swayed slowly amidst the weakness. He could see I was losing strength quickly and his mind was turning to find a way to keep us dancing. He lifted me by my waist and gently set my feet on his while singing in my ear the words from Randy Travis's song "Forever and Ever, Amen."

He began weeping. He was crying harder than I had seen him cry since I had been diagnosed with cancer. It was tender, vulnerable, and true. I had so much I wanted to say, but I just melted into the moment.

I have missed you too, my love. I wish I could stay awake for more than a couple of hours a day. I feel like time is slipping through our fingers while I slowly slip away into someone merely half alive. I promise you I'm fighting with all that I am and all that I have. Please don't let go of me. Please don't give up on me.

As I closed my eyes and buried my head in his chest, I remembered just months ago dancing at the family barbecue we hosted when I was in my sparkly boot before we knew I was sick, the way the music floated on the air accompanied by laughter and the smell of the firepit. Now we found ourselves a thousand miles away, wondering each day if I would even wake up at all.

He carefully lifted me up and set my feet gently onto the rug we stood on. He took extra care when he raised my arm to spin me slowly.

I wasn't wearing a pretty dress. I didn't have any bouncing curls. There was no one else around us in the living room except for two unaffected golden retrievers. It was Wes and me in the full expression of irrevocable, undeniable love for each other.

I was hanging on to Wes while we danced with every ounce of strength I had. He had changed my life and I would spend whatever days I had left on earth trying to reciprocate that love to him. Simply being near him made everything better.

"You know what?" Wes asked me as the song came to an end.

"What's that, babe?" I replied weakly.

"I'd like to take you out," he said as he stepped back and placed my hand in his. He got down on one knee and kissed my knuckles that were folded over his fingers.

"Mrs. Body, may I take you out to dinner?" he asked, looking up toward me.

How can I say no to that? But then again, how can I say yes?

"Yes, you may," I muttered, unsure of how this would work with my level of fatigue.

I carefully put on a sleeveless cotton dress that rested just above my knees in length. It was covered with bright yellow sunflowers so I was able to represent sarcoma cancer. The flowy shape made me happy as I looked down at it. I walked into the bathroom to look in the mirror before meeting him in the living room. I stood there in shock.

I could hardly believe the person that was looking back at me:

Her cheeks were incredibly swollen, her face entirely pale, and the bags under her eyes showed that she was profoundly tired. She had no hair on her head, a swollen red arm, and a catheter hanging out of her chest. The person in the mirror looked only half alive.

The person in the mirror was me.

I rubbed my eyes and stared ahead. I didn't even look like myself anymore. Without even thinking about it, I headed back into the bedroom to put a bandana on my head.

"No, darling," he requested as he met me in the room, taking the bandana from me. "I want to see my wife."

He never felt ashamed of me or as if he needed to hide me from anyone. He loved me just the way I was. I had never known a love like that.

The bandana would stay in my drawer that night.

Wes led me proudly into an elegant Italian restaurant with my arm wrapped in his. We moved slowly and carefully and he was patient with every aching step I made. It felt nice to be out of the house because it had been days since I had left. Even though I was barely awake, Wes was lovely in every way as he made efforts to take photos of us, try to make me smile, and did everything he could to create an extra-special date night.

"I'm nervous," I said to him honestly as we discussed my treatment. "I don't know if I'm going to have much strength for this coming week. It's not even my tough chemo week and I'm already having such a hard time this round."

"We'll do what we always do, babe," he assured me as he held both of my hands between his. "We'll do this together one day at a time."

"You're right," I replied in agreement with him.

When we had finished our meal and paid the check, my stomach was full but my energy level was empty. As he led me to the car, my eyes were only half-opened. I think adrenaline had carried me through the evening, but I was more than ready to go back to sleep. It was a good thing I wasn't driving as I fell asleep in the passenger seat within minutes.

"We're back," Wes said, waking me tenderly as we pulled into the driveway.

"Thank you for still dating me," I muttered with my eyes still closed. "I'll never forget this evening. Next time I'm going to treat *you* to a night out."

"Is that so?" he asked, chuckling as he unbuckled my seatbelt. I nodded my head slowly with a sleepy grin.

"Well, I'm looking forward to it," he said. "For right now, though, let's get you back to bed. You had a big night."

No matter what would become of me, I loved the life I had been able to live. Life wasn't as simple as a quick two-hour movie that was wrapped up neatly with a bow on top at the end. It was messy, challenging, and unexpected. I think that was the best part, though.

Witnessing Wes' extraordinary care and pursuit of me in the hardest season of my life had shown me the power of true love. It was a love that had been tested by our circumstances, yet it shone through all the more. It was the same way I felt about my faith in Christ—the way he pursued me while I was a sinner through his death on the cross just so I could have a relationship with him.

No matter what season of life I found myself in, I knew I was truly and completely loved. The world would one day carry on without me, but while I was in the world I was not alone.

I slept like a rock the following days trying to gain as much physical strength back as I could, but it never felt as if I could get enough rest. Before I knew it, it was time for another round of chemo.

Is my body ready for this?

23

Isolation

I could hardly believe I had finished my eighth dose of chemo. It was halfway through November and we were completing cycle four. The side effects, although taxing, had become a little more predictable. The same progression occurred as usual during this part of the cycle, with taste loss, thrush, breath shortness, acne, nausea, and fatigue. Results from my blood work that morning had shown that my white blood cell count was good. Things appeared to be looking up.

I have only two cycles left. That's only four more times to receive chemo. I can do this.

It was right around lunchtime as I peeked into my parents' refrigerator to find something to eat. I had picked up a Tupperware container of leftovers from the night before when it slipped out of my hands and dropped onto the floor. I was grateful that the lid hadn't popped open, but as I bent down to pick it up, I felt an unfamiliar aching in my stomach.

This is new.

As I gradually stood back up, I set the container back into the refrigerator and placed my hand over my stomach. I was abnormally bloated, and it hurt when I applied pressure to it. Nausea started creeping in and suddenly I wasn't in the mood to eat anything.

"I think I'm going to lie down for a nap," I said to my parents and Wes, who were seated at the kitchen table talking.

"Are you doing okay?" Wes perked his head up from across the room to check on me.

"I'm not feeling too good," I told him. "I'm sure I'll be fine when I wake up."

I curled up in bed underneath the covers and quickly dozed off to sleep.

"What's going on," I gasped in an incoherently high-pitched voice.

Beads of sweat dripped down my face. I turned over and sat up as I felt a pool of perspiration beneath me covering the sheets where I had been sleeping. I rolled over and looked at my phone. Four hours had passed since I had lain down.

"Wes!" I called out while I patted my face dry. He hurriedly entered the room.

"Honey, are you okay?" he asked me while sweat emerged and covered my face. "You don't look like you're feeling good. Hang on. I'm going to get the thermometer."

When he came back into the room, he sat next to me and placed the thermometer under my tongue. Within thirty seconds it began beeping loudly.

"Whoa!" I jumped and it fell out of my mouth onto the comforter. "Sorry—that frightened me. I've never heard it beep like that before."

Wes leaned in to pick it up.

"That's because you have a high fever, Nicole," he told me with concern as he showed it to me.

"What do we do?" I asked him, feeling dizzy and weary sitting in my sweat.

"I'm sorry, Nicole," Wes responded as he placed his hand on my shoulder. "Per our medical team's instructions, we need to take you to the cancer center's emergency room when your temperature is over a hundred degrees."

Wes hurriedly packed a small bag for us in case we were there for a couple of hours. He updated my parents to let them know what was going on and we started making our way to the cancer center's emergency room in Houston.

It just so happened that it was 5:00 p.m., so it took us over two hours in heavy traffic to get there that day. I fell asleep on and off the entire way as the swaying of the stop-and-go traffic strangely rocked me to sleep.

Upon arrival, Wes parked the car and quickly came to my side to help me out of the vehicle. When I went to stand up, I almost fell over. Things had gotten worse over the last couple of hours and I could barely walk on my own at this point.

I thought I had a grip on this. Things had felt a little more predictable this week and were starting to look up. What's happening?

"We'll get you up right away," the woman at the emergency room check-in counter promised.

When we were taken up to the room, it felt as if my stomach had expanded even more. No matter what I did, I was unable to get comfortable and I felt worse and worse as my fever progressed.

Almost two hours after having scans and blood work done, a doctor stood at the door knocking to come in. He had on a faded yellow gown, a blue-and-white mask on his face, and blue gloves on his hands.

"What's going on?" I asked when he entered. I looked back and forth between Wes and him.

"Nicole," he said loudly so I could hear him through his mask, "your test results show that your pancreas is swollen, you have colitis, a UTI [urinary tract infection], and C. diff [Clostridium difficile]. We need to get you admitted into the hospital."

"I'm so sorry—I don't understand," I replied, shocked by the news. "Am I going to be okay?"

"We're going to do everything we can to stabilize you, starting by getting you hooked up to fluids to help you fight this," he replied.

"Am I going into surgery?" I asked with concern. "Is that why you're dressed like that?"

"You're not having surgery right now, but because you have C. diff, you're highly contagious," he educated me. "Whenever someone enters your room, they will be required to wear what I'm wearing now: a gown, gloves, and a mask. We need to make sure your guest puts on this attire right away."

My heart sank to the pit of my pain-ridden stomach. All these new findings were piled on top of sarcoma cancer and a blood clot. I wondered how I could have the strength to fight this off with my body at its weakest point in my fourth round of chemotherapy. If that weren't bad enough already, I had now become a hazard to everyone who came near me.

"How long will I need to stay in the hospital?" I asked, trying to understand how serious things were.

"I'm not sure," he replied in a serious tone of voice.

"Thank you for letting us know." Then a nurse came into the room to transport me to the main building.

The nurse placed a mask, gloves, and a gown on me, and cautiously laid me back down. I watched the ceiling tiles above me while we began moving. I could see Wes out of the corner of my eye walking beside my rolling bed.

When we had made it to the elevator, the nurse pushed the button for the elevator. We happened to stop underneath a mirror that was used to see if someone were coming around the corner.

I took a closer look at it and was stunned when I saw my reflection. The only parts of me that could be seen were my bald head and glazed eyes. The rest of me was fully covered as I lay there in complete stillness.

It looked as if I were dead.

I felt Wes' tender touch on my shoulder, and I shifted my glance at him. A tear rolled down the crease of my eye as I tilted my head toward him.

"I love you," he said, nodding with reassuring eyes. "God is with us right now."

He could have said anything but had chosen the exact words I needed to hear. Since the doctor never gave an estimate of a discharge date, I was unsure if I would even make it out of there alive. I prayed for comfort in the pain, contentment despite my circumstances, and tried to shift my focus on all the reasons I wouldn't give up.

The elevator signal sounded, the doors opened, and I was taken to the floor I would be staying on.

My future had never been more unclear.

24

Leaving a Legacy

Our first night at the hospital had been sleepless. No matter what I did, I couldn't get comfortable and nurses were continually in and out of the room. I felt terrible. In the morning I tried to rest as much as I could to make up for the difficult night.

To our surprise, the door swung open to our patient room and a new nurse said, "Mrs. Body, we're moving you to a different floor for the remainder of your stay."

"Okay," I said, and Wes started gathering our belongings. Everything felt off and inconsistent already, so switching rooms didn't bother me much.

After a few minutes of packing, I put on my isolation attire and the nurse began helping us move to our new room. She made small talk along the way, but as we got closer to the new room she shifted the conversation in a more serious direction.

"Have you ever filled out a power of attorney or a living will?" she asked as we continued down the hallway.

"No," I replied, concerned at her asking this question. "Is that something I need to do?"

"I'll make sure someone comes to discuss it with you when we get you settled in."

Those are end-of-life documents. Did they think—was I—?

Within five minutes of arriving at our new room, a social worker was there to greet us. She asked some basic questions, but I was distracted by the sizable shower that was right behind her. I wanted a moment to get cleaned up after two days in the hospital without a shower.

"Nicole, have you considered completing paperwork for a living will and power of attorney?" she asked me, now gaining my complete attention.

"I don't fully understand what that means," I replied nervously.

"Well, it's a good thing to have completed and stored in our files. These two documents will share your wishes for decisions you'd like to have made if you are ever in a place where you can't make decisions for yourself."

"I'm sorry," I replied, embarrassed of my slowed ability to comprehend. "I'm not sure I completely follow. Could you help me understand a little more?"

"No need to apologize," she said kindly. "For example, if you were in a coma and the medical team knew you would be brain dead if you woke up, these documents would tell us what you would like your medical team to do. It takes the pressure off your loved ones choosing what to do and allows the decision to be made by you right now while you're able to make it for yourself."

"Um," I stammered, looking at Wes. I had never thought of anything like this before. "Yes, I suppose that's something I would like to do. I don't want there to be any stress on my husband if something happens to me."

"All right," she said. "I'll get the paperwork and I'll be right back."

I felt stressed. I wanted to get up and pace, but my stomach hurt too much to walk. I wanted to eat something for comfort, but I was still on a liquid diet. I wanted to cry, but I just didn't have any tears left to give. The only thing I had the strength enough to do was to close my eyes and pray.

> *When you pass through the waters, I will be with you; and through the rivers, they shall not overwhelm you; when you walk through fire you shall not be burned, and the flame shall not consume you.* (Isaiah 43:2)

> *Dear Lord, you are with me—now and forevermore. I'm scared, but I do trust you. Help me keep my eyes on eternity. I always knew we would unite in heaven—I just never thought it might be so soon. Help me to make the best decisions I can to honor and love Wes well.*

The room felt cold. It was surreal filling out the documents.

Six months ago we were traveling and planning for our future together, but now we found ourselves planning for a future apart from each other.

"I brought you something," the nurse said after I finished signing. "This book is called *Celebrating My Legacy.* It will help you in planning activities to celebrate memories and good times with loved ones. It gives you a space to share words that you want to be remembered too."

"Thank you, ma'am," I said, slowly taking the book from her hands. As she exited the room I opened up to a random page. I stared for what seemed like minutes.

"Babe," Wes said, concerned, as he looked over my shoulder, "what is it?"

"It's a page that helps you plan a funeral," I spoke robotically reading the horrific words off the page. "These are the pages that will help prepare my funeral."

"We don't have to do this right now." Wes could see how upset I was.

"No." I stopped him and looked him squarely in the face. "This is important. I filled out the documents to make this easier on you and even though I'm weak, I'm still cognizant enough to help plan this. The less you have to do when the time comes, the less stress you'll have on making these decisions. I can do this."

"Okay," he said as tears welled up in his eyes. I realized how heartbroken he was too. "Where would you like to begin?"

"I would like to be cremated," I told him with difficulty keeping eye contact with him.

"Where would you like your ashes to be placed?" he stammered with every word he said. He took the book from my hands to start writing it down.

"One of three places," I replied without hesitation. I was surprised that I knew so quickly, but I was confident with my answer. "The pond at the Della Terra Mountain Chateau, where we were married if they allow it. If not there, I would like them scattered at the bottom of Manoa Falls in Oahu, where I felt like I had touched heaven with you back in May."

"And the third option?" he asked without looking up as he wrote.

"The third place would be in an urn that remains close to you," I said as tears streamed down my face. "All the best moments in my life have been with you. Although we said, 'Until death do us part,' I feel that part of me will always remain by your side."

He put down the book, crawled into the same tiny hospital bed with me, and held me close. I melted in his embrace as my mind flashed back to all the beautiful memories we had made in this life together. The love that we had was real, and I had understood it more clearly than ever before while battling cancer.

"You have to promise me something, Wes," I said through my tears. "Promise me that you will take my journal entries and share them with the world. Share the words of hope in Christ and the goodness of God that we have witnessed and experienced together. I want patients and people going through hard times to know they aren't alone. Please, Wes. Can you promise me this?"

"I will," he replied as seriously as I had ever heard him speak. "But can I tell you something?"

"Anything," I replied.

"I have a feeling it will be *you* telling this story," he said, lifting my hands to kiss them while nodding his head with vigor. "Don't give up. I know this is hard, but we endeavor forward when things seem impossible. *We* can. *You* can. Your story isn't over yet."

It was as though he had packaged up the most valuable gift in the world and handed it over to me. He had lit a fire in my soul. His words had given me hope and strength that I could keep going.

I started thinking about what I wanted to do with my life: the callings I had pushed aside, the guilt and shame I had carried, and the unhealthy habits I wanted to break.

"Wes, there are a lot of things I want to do differently in life," I said to him as I changed the direction of our conversation. "I want to leave a legacy. I want to write a book, be more intentional about relationships, advocate for patients, and serve others around me. Whether I have a little or a lot of time left, I want to start living well and loving deeply. I want to glorify God and love people with my life."

"I believe you can and will do all of that," he said as the light came back into his eyes. "I'll be right beside you every step of the way."

There was something else I couldn't get off my mind, something I had struggled with for a long time that I was sick of wrestling with.

"I've battled with food for far too long and I don't want to struggle with it anymore," I vulnerably confessed to him. "I want to change my mentality toward food. I want to view it as fuel to keep my body healthy and not mistreat myself by eating too little or too much. If I'm ever able to be off of this liquid diet, will you help me? Will you pray with me?"

"Anything you need from me," he said as he took my hand. "Always remember that I love you no matter what."

He kissed me and got out of the hospital bed to stretch his arms and legs. I felt encouraged by the hope he had shared and my new sense of direction. Although I wasn't feeling good physically, my mind, heart, and soul were uplifted.

Wes reached for the *Celebrating My Legacy* book at the end of my hospital bed and picked it up to place it in our bag.

"Are you going to be okay?" I asked Wes while he held the book in his hands. "If I die, will you be okay?"

"Nicole Madison Body," Wes said as he stopped and sat back down on the bed with me. "Losing you is unfathomable to think about. I don't even think I can fully digest what life on this earth would be like without you. I do know with all my heart that God will see me through it if that day comes before my passing. I will hold on to the hope that I will one day see you again in heaven."

He kissed me on the forehead and looked at me with a steadfastness in his eyes. I felt every word he said to my core and I knew he meant each one.

We would make every day count together until we didn't have anymore.

25

Changed

Yesterday had taken a lot of energy out of me. It was both sad and beautiful as we went through the *Celebrating My Legacy* book and engaged in deep dialogue about the future.

To our amazement, my blood work results looked better the next morning and the bloating in my stomach had gone down. The fluids and medications I was taking were working and I was starting to feel better.

I was finally able to take a shower in the morning, which felt incredible, and I had been taken off the liquid diet by that evening. Recovery was slow-moving, but I was gaining my strength back.

"At this rate of recovery, you might be able to leave tomorrow to continue your recovery at home," the nurse informed us when she entered the room

"Really?" I asked, looking over at Wes. "This calls for a celebration!"

"Oh, yeah," he said, nodding and excitedly shifting to the edge of his seat. "How would you like to celebrate? You name it—we'll do it!"

"Honestly," I told Wes, "I want to take another shower."

"A shower?" he repeated, surprised. "You took one earlier this morning."

I knew it would be an undertaking to prepare me for another

shower. It already took a long time when we were at my parents' house, but in the hospital, where I was hooked up to an IV pole from the CVC line in my chest, the preparation was even longer. We had to be careful and move slowly.

"I know," I said as I expected his reaction to be like that. "The way the warm water feels is so comforting, though, and I would like to take another one if that's okay."

He got everything together to cover my CVC line and grabbed a fresh towel for me to use. I carefully rolled my IV pole beside me toward the bathroom so he could help me get ready.

I took off my shirt and Wes began placing the plastic wrapping on Carl to protect it as he did for every shower. The long IV tube hung out the bottom of my line nearly touching the ground as it looped back up the pole nearby.

"Hang on just one second," he said. "I'm not sure if the door to our room is closed. I'm going to go check real quick."

"Okay," I said as he exited the bathroom.

Since I had already showered earlier in the day, I felt like I had a pretty good grip on what I needed to do. I went ahead and untangled myself from the six-foot-long IV line and bent down to remove one leg from my pants.

That was easy enough. I don't think I'll need Wes' help.

Since the first leg seemed easy to remove, I hurriedly began removing my second leg out of the pants. Being a little more lackadaisical, I looked up to see if Wes was coming back. When I shifted my focus, I started losing my balance. I began hopping on one foot, which caused me to turn and wrap the IV line around my body.

I knew I wouldn't be able to stand on one foot for much longer, so I threw my second pant leg off and slammed my foot down to the floor.

But I had crashed down on more than just the floor.

I ended up stomping on the entangled IV line when my foot hit the floor. It aggressively yanked my CVC line from my chest with the full weight of my body. The pain screamed through the trunk of my body.

Did I just rip Carl out of my chest? Am I bleeding? I can't look.

"Help!" I hollered at the top of my lungs. "Help!"

"Nicole!" Wes came running into the bathroom. "What's wrong? What's wrong? Are you okay?"

"I stepped on the IV line while undressing and felt a rip in my chest!" I yelped, standing there unclothed and shaking. "I think I ripped the stitches out that hold my catheter in, but it's covered so I can't see it! I can't look!"

"My wife is hurt!" Wes called out as he ran out into the hallway. "We need help now!"

The pain was searing and the fear that I could be bleeding caused me to shake all the more. I couldn't bear to look at it in fear that I would pass out, so I closed my eyes and turned my head opposite of where my line was placed. My chest was throbbing and I was mortified.

Within moments three nurses ran into the room to come to my aid. I had never felt so vulnerable and exposed as I hovered my shaking hand over my chest while sobbing.

"It's all right," one of the nurses assured me. "We're here to help. We'll do this very slowly."

They gathered around me and carefully removed the covering from my CVC line. I gritted my teeth and waited to see their reaction. When the covering was removed, I turned back toward their faces to see what they had found.

Each one of them let out a sigh of relief.

"You're okay—it's okay," another one of the nurses said in a calming voice. "You aren't bleeding, but you tugged on the stitches that hold your line in. They appear to be loose. I can see why that scared and hurt you."

"I thought I was going to bleed out and die right here," I confessed to them through my tears. "So many things have been threatening my life lately, but I wasn't expecting to die because of Carl."

"Who's Carl?" the third nurse asked me confusedly.

"Oh, I'm sorry," I said humored by how ridiculous that must have sounded. "We named my CVC line 'Carl.'"

"I see," she replied with a smile. "Well, you're going to be just fine."

"Can I ask a question?" I wiped my eyes as they walked toward the door. "Do people ever actually pull out their CVC lines by accident?"

"They do," she replied, nodding her head. "You're very fortunate that it didn't happen to you. That area will be tender for a few days so continue to be gentle around it. Best of luck to you and 'Carl.'"

As they left I felt exposed, embarrassed, grateful, and shaken all at once. Of the many unexpected twists through cancer treatment, this was one that I couldn't have predicted in a million years. There wasn't a manual titled "How to Handle Issues You May Experience During Cancer: Shower Edition."

I decided to move forward with taking a shower to try calming down. Wes stood in the bathroom close by while I took deep inhalations and let the hot water hit my back.

"Things could have gone very badly," I said to Wes. "I'm sorry I wanted to take a second shower. I'm also sorry I didn't wait for you to help me. I should have known that I wouldn't have been able to keep my balance. I'm not thinking straight."

"It's okay, Nicole," he said while rubbing my back. "I'm sorry this all happened. You've had a tough couple of days. I do hope we get to leave tomorrow. That would be nice."

Wes carefully helped me dry off and get dressed after I finished showering. I was exhausted and my chest was tender where I had pulled on the line.

"If you're up for it, I would love to take you for a walk," Wes offered after we took a few moments to settle down. I realized that the only times I had left the room since I was admitted were when I was transferred or having scans. I was so sick that I hadn't even noticed.

"I would like that," I answered.

We got dressed in full isolation coverings and Wes escorted me to the very top floor of the cancer center. It offered a beautiful view of downtown Houston with the lights of the city shining brightly. Since it was late in the evening, we were the only ones on the observation deck.

"Now this is what I should have initially asked for to celebrate our being discharged from the hospital tomorrow," I said, laughing as he placed his arm around me.

I took a moment to close my eyes while resting my head on his shoulder. When we said, "For better or for worse" three years ago when we got married, I truly believe we meant it.

But how could one fathom what "for worse" would actually look like? Who could know what he or she would face "in sickness"?

I was reminded that this was why we made our vows before God: We would need his direction and guidance for the unexpected turbulent moments like these that would try to rock our world. His love and strength would be the help we needed to see us through. We could always rely on him and trust him to keep our marriage strong.

I felt grateful that we had made it through another crazy day and found ourselves in each other's steadfast arms.

As we headed back down toward our room, I remembered that cycle four would conclude at the end of this week and I would have blood work and scans to assess if the treatment was working.

Whether the state of my tumor had changed or not, I knew that I had changed. Each circumstance that tried to knock me down ended up shaping me, growing me, strengthening me, and giving me greater gratitude for life.

I was shaky, but for now, I was still standing.

26

The News

Beep. Beep. Beep.

It was a never-ending sound from my alarm that I had become all too familiar with.

I had been discharged from the hospital a few days ago to recover back at my parents' house. I was glad not to have an IV pole with me to pull alongside me everywhere I went, especially to accompany me in the shower.

The number of alarms we had to set to remind me to take medication had increased from the additional prescriptions I was given from the visit to the emergency room. Fortunately, my symptoms were being managed and I was feeling better.

We went to the cancer center, where I completed my CT scan and blood work to evaluate how well the treatment was working after the last two cycles. We had experienced positive feedback after the first two that the tumor had shrunk to half the size that it was, but we weren't sure what to expect since there had been a delay in my treatment and the dosage of chemo had been lowered for this cycle.

Thankfully, that day we didn't have to wait very long to be taken back to see Dr. Conley. Leslie came out to the patient waiting room to greet us and took us to one of the rooms in the back.

"Let's talk about your recent visit to the emergency room," she said as she got situated in front of the computer to take notes.

"I don't even know where to start," I told her as I put my hands on my head. "Well, I came down with a fever, triggering the urgency for us to go to the hospital."

There was a knock at the door, and Dr. Conley entered. I was startled since he had never come in before Leslie left at any appointment since I became a patient months ago.

"Leslie," Dr. Conley said to her, "can you come back and work on that with them in a little bit? I'd like to talk with Nicole and Wes now."

"Not a problem," she replied and looked back toward us. "I'll be back in a bit."

"Well, Nicole," he began saying while Leslie closed the door behind her. "I have good news and I have bad news. Which one would you like me to begin with?"

Before I could even think, I blurted out an answer.

"Bad," I said quickly. "I'd like to hear the bad news first."

"Okay," he replied. "The bad news is that your liver levels are spiking again."

"All right," I said, realizing that this would result in another delay of treatment.

"The good news is," he paused and smiled, "even though we lowered your dose of chemo, your tumor has not grown or spread."

I was relieved to hear that the cancer hadn't spread but I had some questions.

"Is my liver going to be okay?" I inquired.

"It should recover with time," he said.

"That's good news," I said thankfully. "What does that mean going forward?"

"Since we have already lowered the dose of chemo from the last cycle and the tumor did not shrink, I do not believe chemo would benefit you moving forward," he said.

"What?" I replied. "So—I'm—I'm finished?"

"You are finished with chemotherapy," he said and clapped in celebration. "Congratulations! You did it!"

I couldn't believe it. I was done with chemotherapy. All the side effects, sleepless nights, and medication would slowly start fading away.

It was the end of the most challenging season for me—a step completed, a milestone to be celebrated.

"This is great news!" Wes said as he came up beside me and hugged me. "What are the next steps for us?"

"Your radiation oncologist shared that the location of your tumor is complicated for radiation," Dr. Conley continued. "Since the tumor is close to your small intestine, we need to deliberate and decide if we will move forward with radiation or if we will move straight to the Whipple procedure."

"Okay," I stuttered. "Okay—okay."

I couldn't even fully digest the excitement of finishing chemotherapy before I was launched back into a fighter mentality with the possibility of radiation and the Whipple procedure approaching quickly.

"When will we hear from you regarding radiation?" Wes asked, standing next to me.

"We will contact you by the end of this week."

"Thanks, Dr. Conley," I said as he stood up to leave.

"I also meant to tell you that we have you scheduled to get your CVC line removed," he told us while standing in the doorway. "You don't need it anymore."

"Oh, that's great!" I replied as the news kept coming in. "Thank you. We'll talk with you soon."

"Sounds good," he replied. "Congratulations on finishing

chemotherapy and let us know if you need anything."

After Leslie came back to conclude our appointment, we said our goodbyes and started heading to the door. When we checked out, I was told that my CVC line removal was scheduled in two days.

"Can you believe you're finished with chemo?" Wes said, jumping up and down in the hallway.

"It's incredible!" I exclaimed. "I know I had two more cycles, but it was clear that my body could not take it anymore."

"How do you feel about saying goodbye to Carl?"

I had been so excited about finishing chemo that I almost forgot how painful it was to have my CVC line placed.

Would it be equally as horrible having it taken out as it was when they put my CVC line in?

"Honestly, I'm pretty terrified," I said, dreading the day it would be removed.

The next couple of days were wonderful. Family and friends cheered and rejoiced with us as we shared the news of the chemotherapy coming to an end. I only had one more step to complete.

The day had come to have my CVC line removed, so we headed back to Wound Care at the cancer center and waited for me to be called back.

I kept trying to tell myself that this was the final closure for chemo and that I could do it. I hoped they would let me listen to worship music again and that it would be quicker to take out than it was to put in. It was evident that I was nervous as I quickly tapped my toes on the floor in the waiting room with Wes.

"Body," I heard a voice call across the waiting room. "Nicole Body."

"That's me," I said, raising my hand and kissing Wes on the cheek.

"We'll talk soon. Say goodbye to Carl!"

"Goodbye, Carl!" Wes said, waving at my CVC line jokingly as I walked back.

I was shaking the sweat from my hands as we walked down the back hallway toward the patient room in anticipation of what was coming. I removed my shirt and laid down so the attendant could access it easily.

"Are you ready?" she asked, moving a chair close to me.

"Is this going to hurt?" I asked her as I turned my head away to avoid seeing what she was doing. All the memories of the insertion came rushing back from the pain, the pressure, and the summoning of the scalpel.

"You'll feel some pressure from the stitches being removed and the line being pulled, but it's nothing like the insertion," she reassured me.

"Okay then," I told her, shutting my eyes. "I'm ready."

She started by pulling the stitches from my chest that held the line in. I took slow, deep breaths through it, feeling only a couple of zings during that step of the removal.

"Now for the line," she said, pushing her entire hand down on my chest. "One, two, three."

A momentary force of pressure emerged. And then nothing happened.

"Is that it?" I asked with eyes still tightly closed.

"That's it," she told me, placing an intense pressure over the spot where my line had been removed. After a few moments, she placed a white bandage over the holes in my chest from the catheter and the stitches.

"You did great," she said.

"That's it?" I asked, laughing with eyes now opened. "I'm free to go?"

"Yes, you are," she said. I thanked her and left.

I came out of the back into the waiting room where Wes was seated. Before I reached him, I pulled down the neck of my shirt showing off the bandage covering the spot where Carl once was. When I got closer to him, Wes reached up and placed his hand gently on the bandage. To my surprise, he began crying.

"Babe," I said as I cupped my hand and placed it over his. "What's wrong?"

"Taking care of Carl has been such a huge responsibility for me over the last four months," he said, staring at our hands atop the bandaged area. "It was a big undertaking for both of us and now Carl is gone. You did it!"

My CVC line had been a huge commitment and investment for Wes. He had taken three hours of classes so he could not only flush it twice a day but also do dressing changes in a sterile environment. He dressed it in gauze for every shower, helped me dress when it was restricting my ability to do so, and attended countless appointments to make sure it was safe and functional for me.

"Wes, you've done so much," I told him with tears in my eyes. "You've worked tirelessly day in and day out on my behalf—not just with Carl but through all of this."

"I love you," he said as he removed our hands from the bandage and kissed the spot right above it.

We spent the hour-long drive back up north processing through emotions and reliving all the crazy adventures we had experienced with Carl. It had been a unique experience filled with terror from the insertion, gratitude for its functionality, the horror when I almost ripped it out of my chest, and the ease in having it removed. We would never forget what life had been like with Carl.

Tomorrow we were scheduled to meet with the radiation oncologist and pancreatic surgeon at the cancer center to find out what my adjusted treatment plan would look like.

As I lay in bed that night, I felt that I was legitimately able to celebrate the end of chemo. Carl was gone and I rested assured, knowing that I could keep going forward.

The only thing we were certain about was that we were in this together.

27

Fourteen

The morning felt like a blur. We had been at the cancer center for hours before meeting with the radiation oncologist. We learned that my name had been the "buzz word" among the panel of providers trying to decide what to do with my case. After extensive discussion, they came to a decision and sent us along to my next appointment.

"You won't believe it," I told Libby over the phone.

"What did the radiation oncologist say?" she asked me with anticipation.

"They're not going to be doing radiation on me," I told her, still shocked repeating the news I had heard moments ago. "We're sitting in the waiting room of the Gastrointestinal Center ready to meet with the pancreatic surgeon to discuss surgery."

"That's big news," she said after a moment of silence. "Will you let me know what the surgeon says when you find out?"

"I will," I promised. "I love you."

"I love you too."

Wes and I took time to text-message the rest of our friends and family with the news we had received.

When we heard my name called, Wes and I headed back with the nurse. After waiting for about twenty minutes in the patient room, we heard a gentle knock on the door and my surgeon walked in.

"Hello," I said. "It's nice to see you, sir."

"It's nice to see you too," he replied as he shook our hands.

"We've been anxiously awaiting this appointment as you can imagine," I said. "We're ready to hear what the next steps are."

"Here's what we plan on doing," he replied as Wes and I shifted to the edge of our chairs. "We would like to move forward with surgery where I will perform the Whipple procedure on you. Everyone agreed that it is the next best step. Let me show you what that will look like."

He turned his back toward us and logged into the computer in the patient room. He clicked on a few icons and we saw a CT scan appear on the screen. He rolled his chair off to the side so we could clearly see the screen while he explained.

"This is your CT scan," he said, circling his mouse around the image. "Here is your sarcoma. When I go in for the procedure, I will remove the tumor, part of your small intestine, and the head of your pancreas. After I do that, I will reattach your pancreas to your small intestine and reroute your intestines. I will likely remove part of your stomach and part of your colon as well to make sure we get all the cancer out."

"I knew about most of that happening," I said slowly as I swallowed a lump in my throat. "The news of removing part of my stomach and part of my colon is new to me, though."

"I will make a vertical incision through your abdomen," he said while motioning the entire length of his abdomen. "This will take around four to six hours for me to complete if there are no complications."

"That seems pretty serious," Wes said, chiming in. "How difficult is the recovery for this?"

"When Nicole wakes up, she'll have a feeding tube, catheter, and a drain in her stomach eliminating fluids from her pancreas," he replied. "She'll likely stay in the hospital anywhere from seven to ten days to recover before being discharged to finish recovering at home."

"Oh, wow!" I said, trying to take it all in.

"One thing that I have to tell you is that there is a percentage of people who do not survive the surgery," he said with a straight face. "I have not lost anyone during the Whipple procedure, but I do need to disclose that there *is* a percentage of people who do die during it."

"Okay," I replied with widened eyes, looking at Wes.

"What is the end goal for this surgery?" Wes asked the surgeon.

"I believe that I'll be able to get all of the cancer out by performing the surgery this way," he replied confidently. "You will be cancer-free after surgery. I can't guarantee that it won't return, but I will get it all out."

"Yes!" Wes shouted loudly.

"It's going to be a long recovery," he leveled with us. "It's a difficult surgery to get you to be cancer-free, but we will get there. I'm confident of that. My nurse will be in shortly and he can help set a date for the surgery."

"Thank you," Wes and I said before he exited the room.

"Cancer-free." That sounds marvelous.

I was certain that this would be the hardest thing I had ever endured, but it was going to be worth it. If all went well, we could potentially be back home in Colorado in a couple of months. I first had to wrap my head around a life-threatening surgery to get there.

The surgeon's nurse walked into the room and brought paperwork regarding the surgery for us to look over. He then pulled up a calendar on the computer.

"Let's see," he said as he scrolled down. "Aha! There we go. On December 13 he has an opening. Does that work for you?"

Wes and I looked at each other, a bit stunned.

"That's in two weeks," I said, raising my eyebrows, creating creases in my forehead.

"Yes," he laughed. "*Does* that work for you?"

"Does it work for us?" I repeated, looking at Wes, who was nodding his head. "Yes, yes it does work for us."

"Okay," he said while he clicked a few buttons and closed out of the screen. "Two weeks it is. I need to grab a couple more papers with instructions, so you have everything you need to prepare for the procedure. I'll be right back."

"Wow!" I said to Wes as we were left alone in the room. "That was a lot of information—both encouraging and intense."

"Are you doing all right?" he asked me while twiddling his thumbs. He was also trying to process it.

"For the most part, I am. It's weird to think that I will either wake up cancer-free or wake up in heaven. How are *you* doing?"

"Fourteen days," he said staring blankly ahead. "I'm thankful that he'll be able to remove the cancer. I hate the idea of you being in more pain or even the thought of losing you. We're going to make the most of these next few weeks and then power through recovery together. I know you can do this."

"I'm certainly going to try," I told him while we sat in momentary silence.

"Why don't we reach out to our friends and family to let them know? Maybe we can even go back to visit them before your surgery."

"That's a great idea," I replied, and we both pulled out our phones to start contacting them.

When I looked at my phone I saw a list of text message responses from the update we had sent before the appointment. As I started replying and sharing the news, a message from my friend Jenna caught my eye.

"Are you allowed to go to Disneyland before you have radiation or surgery?" it read. "My family would like to send us there with all expenses paid if you can go."

I smiled big and started laughing out loud at the idea of going to

Disneyland. I had never been before and it had been a dream of mine to go, but I was fresh off of chemotherapy and a recent emergency room visit.

Could I go to Disneyland right now?

"What is it?" Wes asked, looking up from his phone.

"Well, Jenna asked if I could go to Disneyland with her before surgery. Her parents want to send us there together with all expenses paid! Do you think they would be okay with me going? Would *you* be okay with me going?"

"Of course—I would be more than okay with that!" he exclaimed. "That's generous and sounds like a blast. We can ask the nurse when he gets back."

The nurse walked back in and left the door cracked open while he handed us the rest of the paperwork. We placed it into the folder and put it into our bag to take to my parents' house with us.

"Did you have any other questions?" he asked, looking at both of us.

"Could you ask the surgeon if I'm allowed to go to Disneyland before surgery?" I asked with a goofy grin on my face. "My friend's family has offered to send us there for a couple of days. If it's okay with my team, I'd like to go."

"You *should* go," I heard a voice say from the hallway. When I looked up, I saw my surgeon peeking through the doorway with a big grin. He must have heard me ask while he was walking by.

"All right!" I replied to him and smiled at Wes. "That's awesome!"

There was a lot to look forward to over the next two weeks. We made plans to visit friends in Dallas, family in Colorado, and I now had a trip planned to Disneyland with Jenna.

These next two weeks were important, and I wanted to be intentional with the time spent with loved ones. The Whipple procedure was going to be life-threatening and if I survived it, it would be life-changing. My life was going to change dramatically one way or another in fourteen days.

The countdown to surgery had officially begun.

28

The Letter

"What was your favorite memory from the last two weeks?" Wes asked me in my parents' living room. "It had to be visiting Disneyland."

"Disneyland was incredible," I told him. "I'll remember it and cherish it forever. However, I have to say that *all* of it was wonderful."

"Really?" he replied in shock. "Disney is your favorite thing in the world. Disneyland is called 'the happiest place on earth.' I didn't think anything could compete with that."

"I know," I replied in laughter. "Seeing friends in Dallas and Colorado was great too. And we got to celebrate an early Christmas with both of our families. It was an amazing two weeks. I can't choose a favorite because it was all special and meaningful.

"That's a great problem to have," he laughed. "I'm glad you enjoyed it all."

Surgery was scheduled for the very next day and we had spent the last couple of days getting organized and packed so we were ready to go. The day had flown by and we were spending time with my family before turning in for the night.

"So, Nik," my dad said, waving at me to meet him in the kitchen,

"I wanted to let you know that I'm happy to clear my calendar to perform your upcoming surgery."

"Oh, yeah?" I asked, laughing after I got up and met him there. "And your credentials?"

"Well, it's all in the name, really," he said as he walked near the utensils. "I am Dr. Knife. Dr. Rusty Knife."

"That's funny," I laughed with my head in my hands. "There's not a chance in this world that I would ever be okay with *that* happening!"

"Okay, okay," he said as he raised his hands with a smirk and stepped back. "You just let me know. I've never failed at a surgery."

"Have you ever actually performed one?" I asked sarcastically.

"Nope," he said confidently as he shook his head. "Zero for zero is still one hundred percent!"

"I'll be sure to keep that in mind," I snickered.

We laughed through our nerves more often than not. I had a lot on my mind, but I wanted to try enjoying the evening before my life would be changed tomorrow. Wes got up from the couch and sat down at the kitchen table near where I was standing.

"How are you, sweetheart?" Wes asked me.

"I'm doing okay right now, actually," I told him as I walked toward him to sit down at the table. "I think I just have a lot on my mind leading into tomorrow."

"Why don't you write something? That always brings you joy and calms you down."

"I'm not even sure what I would write."

"What if you wrote a letter?" he said, shrugging his shoulders.

"That's a good idea. Did you have someone in mind for me to write to?"

"I don't know," he said while trying to think of ideas. "You could write a letter to God, to me, or even to one of your doctors. If you write to someone who's associated with the surgery tomorrow, it might help you funnel your thoughts and allow you to process your feelings."

And then it hit me. I knew exactly what I was going to do.

"What if I wrote a letter to *cancer*?" I asked him hoping that he liked the idea.

"I think that's a great idea!" he said with enthusiasm. "I'll give you some space to write. I love you."

"I love you too."

I found a pen and paper and sat back down at the table to write my letter.

Okay, cancer—this one's for you. And believe me—I've got a lot to say.

Dear cancer,

You showed up earlier this year uninvited, unannounced, and unexplained. You disguised yourself outside my pancreas with no intention of being found. No symptoms, no side effects, and you didn't even leave a hint in my blood work. You must think you're clever.

But cancer, we found you.

We went after you since God led us to find you through my gallbladder failing and by moving in the spirit of Dr. Odekirk. This was not an accident. There are no accidents with my God.

You caused me to feel emotions I've never experienced, face fears I didn't want to face, endure pain I didn't know was possible, and you drove me to fight for my life like there was no tomorrow.

Here's the thing, though, cancer: I don't report to you. I am not identified by you. I am not controlled by you. Every ache, pain, tear, and fear cannot keep me down because

Jesus Christ lifts me up. God has used every bit of this to grow my faith, courage, and relationships more than ever.

Cancer, you can't have my spirit. You can't have my soul. You can't have my joy. You can't have my hope. And tomorrow—

Cancer, you are out of here!

I know you'll want to come back. And you might. But if you do, I won't have to fight you alone. Have you met Wes? My family? My friends? My God? They're the ones who have walked with me, lifted me, encouraged me, and loved me. My heart is overflowing. And you'll never win. Because no matter what happens, I have—

Support unshakable,

Love unconditional,

Eternal life unbreakable,

Joy unfathomable,

Laughter uncontainable,

Memories unforgettable,

Faith unstoppable.

So, cancer,

Today and every day, you're just a puny little "c."

And you just aren't a match for my big "C": Christ.

All the other men, women, and children you're messing with? We are never going to give up until we end your presence forever. We will fight together for a cure.

And the ones who have been laid to rest? We hold memories of them close to our hearts. They live on through the lives of loved ones marching on.

Which reminds me, cancer: Even if I don't live past my surgery tomorrow, you don't get the final say. You won't get the victory.

I will.

I will either be cancer-free here on earth or cancer-free in heaven. Regardless, your residence inside me ends tomorrow.

Tomorrow I will be cancer-free.

You may have come to wreak havoc and destruction, but we saw past that and united through our commonalities as patients and became family. You made a mistake by bringing us together because we are going to tear you apart.

We will never give up.

We will never stop fighting.

We will continue praying.

We will continue loving.

You thought you could come in and steal my joy, kill my enthusiasm, and destroy my life, but I found over the last few months that you have great limitations. You are no match for my God, you don't hold a candle to my Wes, and your efforts have been squashed out by the love and loyalty of the people who surround me.

You tried to push me beyond my limits, but you have failed because my God is greater than you. You need to hear that from me.

So, cancer, just a heads-up: My surgeon is sending you an eviction notice tomorrow. And all the researchers, doctors, surgeons, and medical teams in the world will never stop working to get rid of you for good.

I will be cancer-free tomorrow. And no amount of pain, stitches, and tubes can take that joy away from me. Not even death can hold my body down for one day. I will soar the heavens with no pain, sorrow, or disease.

Love has broken through.

Love has won.
Love will always win.
Hoping never to house you again,
Nicole Madison Body

29

Rolling Away

I picked up my Bible from the nightstand next to the bed.

Fear not, for I am with you; be not dismayed, for I am your God; I will strengthen you, I will help you, I will uphold you with my righteous right hand. (Isaiah 41:10)

I needed to read those words because the morning of the Whipple procedure had arrived.

It was still dark outside. Everyone in the house woke up at 4:30 a.m. to get ready. Wes and I packed our remaining toiletries into our suitcase for the predicted ten-day stay at the cancer center. My parents followed us in their car behind us as we began the hour-long drive to Houston. Since it was early in the morning, we made it to the cancer center in record time.

"This is really happening," I whispered to Wes while we walked up to check in.

"It really is," he said.

Three years of undiscovered gallbladder pain had led to the discovery of the cancer. Months of chemotherapy led me to be ready for this surgery.

I wonder if in some ways I've been preparing for this my entire life.

Text messages flooded our phones while we sat in the waiting room. Friends and family woke up early to send words of encouragement and prayers before I went back for the procedure. I looked to my left and my right and was incredibly grateful that my parents and Wes were here beside me.

Deep breaths, Nicole. Keep taking deep breaths.

"Mrs. Body?" I heard a nurse call my name from across the waiting room.

It caught me off guard since we had barely even sat down. But it was time.

The four of us headed back to the pre-surgery room with the nurse. Within moments two anesthesiologists showed up. After a minute went by, a surgeon walked in. I was surprised that it wasn't the one we had previously met with.

"Hi," he said, shaking my hand. "I'm one of three surgeons who will be in the operating room for your surgery today. It's nice to meet you."

Do I need two anesthesiologists and three surgeons for this procedure?

I shook his hand and introduced myself.

I looked around and observed that there were seven people packed inside the room with different moods, expressions, and side conversations happening. It felt as though the walls were closing in.

For the first time in my life, I felt claustrophobic.

My mom smiled at me with hope in her eyes. My dad was intensely listening to what the anesthesiologists said among each other. Wes sat close to me and grazed his fingertips lightly over the palm of my hand to help me relax.

A second surgeon walked in, introduced himself to me, and asked how I was doing.

"I'm not sure," I responded nervously.

I could feel my heart rate rising. There were now eight people in this tiny room. I was trying not to panic—but anxiety was rising within me.

"Ouch!" I yelped as a needle sunk into my left arm. One of the anesthesiologists was starting to prep me for surgery unbeknownst to me. Immediately I had an onset of nausea like nothing I had ever experienced before.

"Oh, wow," I said, covering my mouth. "What was that? I think I'm going to be sick."

"You'll be getting this shot in your arm twice a day to protect your pancreas after surgery," the other anesthesiologist said to me.

"Will I feel nauseated like this every time?" I asked, hoping he would say no.

"Yes," he said with an apologetic look on his face.

In addition to that, he told me that blood thinner meds via shots in my stomach would be administered daily after the surgery. I kept learning new details that were unsettling.

After learning this information from the anesthesiologist seated beside me, I felt movement with the blanket down by my feet.

I shifted my gaze to the end of the hospital bed. Someone new had entered the room and was placing large boot-like devices on my legs.

"What are those?" I asked.

"These are intermittent pneumatic compression devices," she replied. "They'll help prevent blood clots during the surgery."

I felt hot and started breathing hard. I couldn't tell if I was more ill from the shot in my arm or from the number of people in the room. With everything going on around me, I was starting to comprehend the severity of the surgery.

"I've put together a 'cocktail' to administer through your IV," one of the anesthesiologists joked with me. "You'll be asleep very soon after I give it to you in a little while."

After ten minutes had passed and most of the medical team and doctors had stepped out of the room, I looked around and saw my family gathered around me making me feel safe and secure. I wanted some time alone with them before I was taken back for surgery.

"All right," a nurse said, surprising me as she entered the room. "It's time to say your goodbyes."

Oh, no—please, not yet. I need a minute. I'm not ready to say goodbye. I've barely said hello.

I made eye contact with each of my family members and it put my heart at ease. I could see the love they had for me and it helped me relax.

"Good night," my dad said nervously but accomplished his goal of bringing a smile to my face.

"Dr. Knife," I said with forced laughter as my eyes welled up with tears, "you aren't coming back with me?"

"Not today, Nicole Madison," he said quickly while looking away so I wouldn't see him cry. My comedic father had a tender side too, and today I almost witnessed him cry for the third time in my life.

"I love you both," I said to my parents.

"I love you, Nicole," my mom said as she used all her strength to hold it together while she kissed me on the forehead.

"I love you," my dad said, catching my gaze and rubbing his eyes.

The nurse walked beside my bed and started rolling me out of the room. I sat up and turned around to look at Wes. I hadn't said goodbye to him yet. There was no way that I could leave without his hearing that I loved him.

"Please wait," Wes requested as he jumped out of his chair and placed his hand onto the hospital bed I was in. "Can I please pray for her before she goes with you?"

"Of course," the nurse said as she stopped rolling the bed. I was still shaking as I grabbed his hand. I thanked God that I was able to hold it one more time.

"Dear Lord," Wes said, holding my hand with a firm grasp. "Please be with Nicole during surgery. Please guide her surgeons and the entire surgical team."

I felt a sudden calm cover my body as he continued with his prayer.

"And God," he pleaded while sniffling, "please bring my wife back to me."

Tears reactively spilled from my closed eyes.

"Are you ready?" the nurse asked me kindly.

"I am," I said even though I wanted more time. Wes kissed me on the lips and lingered there for as long as he could until it was time for me to go.

When she began rolling my bed away, I locked eyes with Wes and smiled at him until he fell out of my sight. Then the hallway was the only thing I could see in front of me.

My family will be waiting for me on the other side of this. I can do this. I wonder how bad this is going to hurt when I wake up. If I wake up. Don't go there. I've got this. God's got this. I have been given a spirit not of fear but of power and love and self-control.

"Now this room we are heading to will be intimidating," the nurse said, giving me fair warning as she rolled me down the hallway. "My advice is to take deep breaths and focus on the medical staff talking to you. We're going to make a quick stop into this room before we head to the surgical room for you to meet everyone else."

"Okay," I said lightly.

How bad could this room be?

We rounded the corner and there it was. This room was even smaller than the previous one I was in, and it was filled with machinery and black wires from the ceiling to the floor. It covered almost every inch of the room. There was barely enough space to roll my bed inside it or allow anyone else to enter.

I remembered the nurse's advice and stopped looking around. I shifted my focus onto the people who were sharing information with me.

"Would you like a relaxing medication while you wait?" someone new from the medical team asked me.

"Is it that obvious?" I asked through an anxious breath. "That would be nice. Thank you."

"I'll put that in your IV right now," she said sweetly as she could see the nerves building through my eyes. "How's that?"

"Well," I blinked slowly and responded groggily. "It's working."

"Oh, good!" she said. "Let me know if you need anything else.

"My husband," I said as I began growing tired. "I need my husband."

"Actually," she replied, "it will be just a little bit before they take you back. I'm happy to go grab him for you."

"Really?" I asked, facing her with eyelids that struggled to stay open with the new medication I had been given.

I was so out of it that when Wes arrived, I forgot she had even gone to get him. He held my hand and looked at the nurse and laughed.

"You put her on something since I last saw her," he said while they chuckled together.

"Yes," she replied with a smile. "She seems to be doing well, though."

"I am," I chimed in as my smile appeared at the speed of a sloth. "It's for the best, though. This room is like a scene from a scary movie."

Wes looked at me as I began fading away.

"They're having me go now," he whispered to me as he gently tilted my chin up toward his face.

"Wait," I said, trying to process what he had said. "Didn't you just get here?"

"I'm right here with you," he said as he put his hand on my heart.

My emotions overpowered the medication and my eyes began

tearing up.

"You know what, sweetheart?" he said. "You look just as beautiful right now as you did on our wedding day."

"I love you so much," I groggily said, puckering up to kiss him.

"I love you too," he replied and then kissed me and stepped back slowly. I hung on to the tips of his fingers until he was too far from my grasp.

And then he was gone. This time it was for real.

"I know you miss him already," a nurse said as she knelt down beside me. "We're going to take you to the surgical room right now."

"I do miss him," I said with my eyes closed. "Thank you for bringing him back for me to say goodbye again. That was sweet."

"You're welcome," she replied. "Will you be able to help shift your body from this bed to the surgical table?"

"Yes," I replied.

"Okay—here we go," she said to me as we started down the hallway. "That comment he said about your wedding day was sweet. I bet that was a lovely day, wasn't it?"

"It was the best," I responded as I started getting lost in a daydream.

I could hear the words in my head as I was half asleep:

> *"I have told you these things, so that in me you may have peace. In this world you will have trouble. But take heart! I have overcome the world."* (John 16:33, NIV)

It was like an umbrella on a rainy day. And just like that, I wasn't afraid anymore.

"Here we are," she said as I barely opened my eyes while coming out of my thoughts.

The room was huge and chalk white. It was cold and numerous people were organizing and preparing it like machines. Everyone had a task and did it silently and diligently in preparation to operate on me. Even though I was out of it, I detected the grandness of what was about to happen.

This is it. Moments away.

"The room looks very sterile," I observed.

"It *is* very sterile," my nurse reassuringly said as she raised my bed up next to the table where surgery would be performed. "All right—this is where I need your help. Let's get you to slide on over there."

As soon as I got onto the table, my anesthesiologist came over to see me.

"I have that 'cocktail' I told you about earlier," he said to me. "Are you ready for it?"

"Yes," I said. "I am."

"Great," he said to me, lightly holding on to my arm where the IV line was placed. "It's time. Good night."

And the room went black.

30

Awake

Beep . . . beep . . . beep . . .

I could feel the breath coming in and out of my nostrils. The cool air chilled my face as the rest of my body was bundled tightly underneath a blanket. I was too weak to open my eyes.

Is it over? Did I survive the surgery?

I was trying to capture the thoughts softly floating around my head, but I was completely disoriented and couldn't hold focus for long.

Beep . . . beep . . . beep . . .

The beeping noise reminded me of the machine that measured heart rate and blood pressure from previous hospital visits. I wanted to see where it was coming from, so I mustered every ounce of strength I had to open my eyes.

Everything was out of focus as I was coming out of anesthesia and my contacts weren't in. I located the machine that tracked my heart rate and blood pressure but I wasn't in a normal patient room. There were curtains on all sides of me.

I think I'm in a post-operative room. I think I made it. I'm alive.

I closed my eyes again and was easily convinced that a celebratory nap would be a worthy way to spend the next few hours.

Before I faded into slumber, I heard voices that I recognized. They were getting louder as they approached where I was lying down.

I heard the curtain that led to the entrance of the room slide open. I lifted my eyes to see that Wes and my mom had walked in.

I didn't know if I would ever see them again after I had said goodbye before surgery. In response to my best efforts to smile, they started laughing since my motor skills were slower than usual. They immediately launched into conversation with me in hopes that I would become more aware.

"Did you hear?" Wes asked through a tone of excitement that I had never heard in him before. I looked at him to see him vigorously nodding his head. I then glanced over at my mom, who was smiling bigger than I had ever seen.

"Am I cancer-free?" I asked Wes, hoping that was the cause for all the excitement.

"Yes!" he exclaimed. "You are cancer-free, Nicole!"

"Really?" I asked as I closed my eyes again. "I can't believe it. This is the best news. Praise God."

I had made it. I was alive and I was cancer-free.

I was still on so much pain medication that I couldn't feel my body, but my heart was singing.

"Nicole, there's more," Wes continued as I opened my eyes again to look at him. I noticed tears were now rolling down his face. He had a wide-eyed smile and was bursting at the seams to tell me something.

"More?" I asked him in confusion. "How could there be more than that? That was the best possible outcome, wasn't it?"

"She doesn't know," my mom said, gazing over at Wes as they both covered their mouths with their hands.

"What's going on?" I asked with my eyes now fully open looking back and forth at each of them.

"You were in surgery for about two hours." my mom said excitedly.

"We were all sitting together back in the waiting room and I happened to look over toward the front desk. I was shocked that I saw one of your surgeons standing there."

"Wait." I stopped her as I started regaining consciousness a little more. "A surgeon wasn't in the operating room with me?"

"No, he wasn't," my mom replied, shaking her head. I was confused and becoming more alert with every word that was being shared with me.

"I looked over at him and then back at your father and Wes," she continued. "I had the same question: 'Shouldn't he be with Nicole right now?' We made eye contact with him and he called us up to talk to him."

"As soon as we walked up, your surgeon looked over to me and said, 'I have some surprising news,'" Wes continued, sharing what had happened. "We didn't know what to think."

"Then what happened?" I asked while hanging onto their every word.

"He said that they had made the incision in your abdomen and the team went inside to remove the cancer off your pancreas," Wes continued. "But when they went to the spot where the cancer showed up on your scan, they couldn't find sarcoma cancer anywhere."

"Wait, what—?" I asked in shock. "There wasn't any cancer there?"

"The medical team spent the next couple of hours looking for the cancer and even compared it to your last CT scan from a couple of weeks ago," my mom said with uncontainable excitement. "They contacted the radiologist to confirm the location and looked for two hours, but there was no cancer inside you, Nicole. None at all!"

"This doesn't make any sense," I said, convinced that the anesthesia was messing with my head. "Can you tell me again what happened, please?"

"Nicole," Wes said as he knelt down beside me, now fully in tears. "You didn't have to have the Whipple procedure. You were opened up for surgery and the cancer was gone. They closed you back up and now you're here with us."

"So I'm cancer-free?" I repeated with tears in my eyes while he was kissing my hand.

"You are," my mom replied as she walked on the other side of me, leaning in for a gentle hug as she was crying too.

"No organs were removed," Wes shared. "You don't have a feeding tube or a drain coming out of your stomach either. The only thing we're waiting for is the pathology from a small sample of tissue that was in the spot where the cancer was 'supposed to be.' They just want to make sure there weren't any stray cancerous cells that got away."

"Is this all a dream?" I asked.

"This is not a dream," Wes said, laughing through cries. "You have been cured of cancer through a combination of the amazing care you received here and a true miracle from God!"

"A *miracle,*" I said softly as I beheld the word.

"You are a living miracle," my mom said back to me.

"Is Dad here?" I asked. "Does he know?"

"Yes," my mom replied. "Everyone knows! We've contacted friends and family to tell them this incredible news. You're actually the last one to find out."

"So I didn't have the Whipple procedure?" I asked again to clarify once more.

"No, you did *not,*" Wes said in amusement that I wasn't fully processing it.

"Wow!" I said. "This is astonishing. I am speechless."

A nurse poked her head into the room and looked over at me.

"Your patient room is ready, and we're going to take you to it if you're ready," she said with a smile and two thumbs up.

"Absolutely," I responded.

It all felt like a dream while I was wheeled to the room I would stay in for recovery.

Dear God, thank you. I have no other words except that you are my rescuer and I am eternally grateful for you. You never left my side for even a second and you sent me a loving husband, supportive family, incredible friends, and an exceptional medical team to help save my life. In my struggles, fears, and doubts, you love me anyway. Thank you, Jesus. In your wonderful name, I pray. Amen.

When we arrived at the room, my mom immediately started hanging up Christmas decorations all around it. She covered it with small lights and set up a tiny green Christmas tree to make the room festive for the holiday. It felt as if we were celebrating a second Christmas together with the joy that filled the room.

As the day carried on I became exceedingly tired and was ready to rest. I said goodbye to my family and started drifting off to sleep. Wes sat right next to me and took phone calls, sent messages, and emailed updates of what had happened. He read messages to me and rubbed my arm for what seemed like hours.

As I snuggled up under the blanket, I knew there was no dream I could ever have that would be greater than the reality I was living.

We weren't fully in the clear yet, though. We had to wait for the pathology results from the tissue that was taken during surgery before we knew for sure that I was cancer-free.

31

Believe

It had been a beautiful morning. I finally had enough energy and clarity of mind to speak to friends and family by replying to messages and returning phone calls. Some people cried and others were in shock. The resounding exclamation that escaped almost everyone's mouths was "That's unbelievable!"

We were getting close to finding out if it was indeed "believable" since it still wasn't one hundred percent confirmed that I was cancer-free. We were waiting for the pathology report to come back telling us if the tissue my surgeon removed had any cancer cells in it. Although the tumor had miraculously disappeared, the medical team wanted to check to make sure they didn't miss any stray cancer cells. We were waiting eagerly for my surgeon to come by and tell us the news.

Hours had passed and we finally heard a knock on the door.

Could this be my surgeon delivering the news?

I felt my palms start sweating.

"Come in," I said as the door opened.

There was a large group of men and women of various ages gathered around the doorway peeking inside. Each one was holding a stack of papers in his or her hands and was smiling in at us. Wes stood up and went to the door.

"Hi—we are volunteers here at the cancer center," the guy standing in front said. "We would like to sing you a Christmas carol if that would be okay."

"Really?" I asked in shock. "Yes, yes—I would love that."

Every time someone had knocked on my door, it had been for blood work, testing, results, and checks. This was the first time people had come to my door solely for the sake of encouraging me and lifting me up.

"What would you like us to sing?" one of the volunteers asked.

"How about 'We Wish You a Merry Christmas'?" I asked. All of the volunteer carolers flipped the pages of the papers in their hands to find the song.

"One, two—one, two, three, four," the leader of the group said, and they started singing.

"Wes, can you help me up?" I whispered.

After Wes helped me up to standing, I took my IV pole and wheeled it toward the door to get a closer look. I had never experienced something so refreshing. I stood there with my eyes closed taking in the voices harmonizing the cheery song lyrics.

After their performance concluded, Wes and I clapped our hands and thanked them.

"Merry Christmas," their voices lifted in a jovial unison.

"Merry Christmas," we echoed back, and Wes closed the door.

"That's what I want to do," I told Wes as he started walking beside me toward the bed.

"What's that, Nikki?" he asked.

"I want to volunteer like that. I want to love people in remarkable ways like our family, friends, coworkers, and strangers have loved us. I want to be more intentional about my faith, relationships, and serving others. When I'm healed enough to do so, can we do that together?"

"I'm one hundred percent in," he replied, giving me a gentle hug as we stood at the edge of the bed.

Before I could sit back down, I heard another knock on the door.

"Hey—maybe it's the carolers back for round two," I laughed as Wes went to open the door.

It was my surgeon.

He poked his head in and looked around the room before stepping inside.

"I like what you've done to the place," he said, observing the Christmas decorations as he entered. "How are you today?"

"I'm doing well," I replied. "It's good to see you."

"You as well," he said while shifting the conversation. "Well, I have some news for you."

We had reached a crossroads and the next words that came from his mouth would determine the direction of our future.

"I'm ready," I said as Wes moved even closer to me holding onto my arm.

"The pathology came back benign," he said, shrugging his shoulders. "You have no evidence of cancer."

"Really?" I exclaimed. "I'm cancer-free?"

"Yes, you really are," he replied. "I like all the decorations, but don't get too comfortable here. You'll be discharged in a couple of days."

"Wait," I paused while looking at him and then back at Wes. "I'll be out of the hospital by Christmas?"

"You'll be home with lots of time before Christmas," he said to me, nodding his head. "Now rest well and take care of yourself."

"Thank you," I said while he exited the room.

"Wes!" I exclaimed. "This is real. It's all real. It's a miracle. I'm cancer-free. I'm alive. I'm alive!"

"You get to stay with me," Wes said, crying as he wrapped his hand around my bald head, pulling me in closer. He was shaking while holding me tightly as if he would never let me go.

I looked at him tenderly with grateful eyes. He didn't just speak the words he vowed to me years ago—he lived them.

"What is it, honey?" Wes asked me as we looked at each other.

"Thank you for meaning the words you said to me on our wedding day," I said. "I'm not sure either of us could have known what was ahead but you handled it all with such grace. You've shown loyalty and love in the purest form. The foundation of faith you've led this family with will stand firm through whatever else may come in the future. I can never say this enough: I am fully and completely yours 'until death do us part.' I love you."

"I love you so much," he said back to me.

I remembered thinking when I was diagnosed with cancer that he didn't sign up for this. I wondered how I could have asked him to make the sacrifices he made to help me fight this.

It turns out that I didn't have to ask—he just did it.

He left his family, put his career on hold, relocated out of state, sold his truck, drove me to countless appointments, helped me recover through multiple surgeries, went through training on how to change and clean my CVC line daily, lost sleep in my many restless nights, spent days in the hospital, cooked and cleaned for me, held me up and danced with me, made me laugh when I wanted to cry, prayed for me, read to me, encouraged me, listened to me, and more.

Wes loved me.

His love reflected compassion, sacrifice, and commitment. He had chosen me every single day before and during cancer. He never gave up on me and taught me never to give up on myself. I had respect, love, trust, and loyalty toward him and I knew the rest of my life would be different because of the love he had demonstrated to me. It was a love that had been born from great trial and even greater faithfulness from God.

"You know what I can't help but think about at this moment?" he asked me.

"What's that, sweetheart?" I questioned curiously.

"I don't have to keep my promise," he said, smiling big.

"What promise?" I asked, furrowing my brow, unsure of where he was going with this.

"Your journal entries," he explained. "The ones you asked me to share. *You're* going to be the one to tell the story. Throughout this entire journey, God has filled you with light in the darkness, love indescribable, and a message of hope. In addition to everything He did, He even gave you a glorious final chapter: He sent you a true miracle from heaven."

"You're right," I told him, realizing the beauty of this truth. "By the grace of God, I *do* get to share this story."

"I bet He already has your next book in mind," he told me while pinching my chin and winking at me. "Your story isn't over yet."

"Whatever comes next," I replied with a smile. "I can't wait to write about it."

Epilogue

Two days later I was released from the hospital. Being able to attend a Christmas Eve service that year moved my heart and soul in every way. I cried tears of joy and gratitude celebrating the birth of Jesus and the miracle God had performed in my life.

Years later, Wes and I now permanently reside in The Woodlands, Texas. I made a full recovery from surgery and chemotherapy and I am seen every four months by the MD Anderson Cancer Center to do surveillance on the area where my sarcoma cancer was located. So far each report has brought back news of seeing no evidence of disease.

I wear a very large red scar down the center of my abdomen from surgery. We call it my "miracle mark." It has become my favorite part of my body. I'm daily reminded of the great miracle that occurred years ago and how nothing is impossible with God.

With the redirected purpose God revealed to me through cancer, I have pursued writing, blogging, and speaking as a way to communicate, connect, and bring encouragement to others. I'm currently working on two new books and I look forward to what God has for me in the future.

Since I became cancer-free, Wes has worked hard to pursue God's calling in his life. Recently he was given the opportunity for a career change and is now working as a crisis care pastor at our church. He is halfway through his Master of Divinity Degree at Denver Seminary and hopes to pursue his doctorate upon completion of that.

The way our family and friends loved us, coupled with the day that the volunteer carolers came to visit us in the hospital, really changed our outlook on life and encouraged us to volunteer.

We have volunteered at a children's hospital, the MD Anderson Cancer Center, and we participate in cancer fundraisers throughout the year. We had the privilege of visiting the United States Capitol in Washington, D.C., to participate in the One Voice Against Cancer Lobby Day, thanks to a sponsorship from the Sarcoma Foundation of America. We have fully committed to never stop fighting for a cure. Until the day a cure comes, we will promote advocacy, funding, research, and education to help patients across the country and around the world to end cancer.

The commitment to nutrition that we prayed about in the hospital truly transformed our lives and has lasted over the years. For the first time in my life, I do not feel chained down by an addiction to food. Wes and I have lost a total of one hundred thirty-five pounds together in a healthy way and have loved each other through every minute of it. Although my hair has grown back, I'm not attached to it in the way I was before. This was all possible because of the goodness and freedom given to us by God. I finally see myself the way that God sees me.

I was told that I was nearly infertile after my treatment, which was heartbreaking to both Wes and me. After two years of being cancer-free, we were given clearance to try having a baby naturally, but we were told it would be challenging. Wes and I are overjoyed to report that we are currently pregnant with a little girl, Aurora Elizabeth Body!

I grew up in church and always believed that miracles had happened, but I wasn't cognizant that they were still happening today. I certainly didn't believe that one would happen in my life. God opened my eyes through cancer and helped me to see the beauty in creation, people, and even within myself. Miracles are happening all around us every day if we only have the eye to look for them and the heart to truly see them.

My goal is to take God out of the tiny box that I put him in. He is truly immeasurable and so much greater than I could ever fully grasp. I will never stop praising and thanking him for his love and the life he has given me. I am humbled and brought to my knees in gratitude and joy. All glory, honor, and praise belong to him.

Whether my story continues on earth or I leave this world for heaven, my heart is forever full.

I will always remember the time *when love broke through*, knowing that it will do so again and again.

Acknowledgments

First and foremost, I thank the love of my life, Wes Body. I cannot imagine having gone through cancer without you. You are my best friend, caregiver, and the leader of our home through faith in Christ. I never knew I could love someone the way I love you. You loved truly and unshakably lived out your vows before, during, and after our season through cancer together. I know all this was possible because of God's work through you. I have all the respect and love in the world for you. I have come to know Jesus more deeply because of how you live your life. Thank you.

There are not enough words to express my gratitude to Certa Publishing for their willingness to publish my story. You have changed my life by allowing me to dive into my calling. Your love, prayers, attentiveness, and encouragement are etched within the pages of this book.

My mom and dad sacrificed so much for us during treatment. You housed us, shared your dogs with us, and let me run up your water bill for my daily baths during the months we spent there. We could not have had the amazing treatment we did at the MD Anderson Cancer Center without your hospitality.

Kathy and Bode, your love and encouragement lifted us the entire way through cancer and gave us wings on which to soar. Some of my favorite moments to remember and write about are ones that include you in them. Thank you for loving me like your own daughter.

Libby and Randy Hellinger, you are two of the most exceptional leaders of faith, love, and wisdom I have ever known. Your generosity, sacrifice, and encouragement have changed our lives forever. If we can be like any two people in the world when we grow up, we want to be like you. You are the greatest mentors and friends in the universe.

I have been blessed with exceptional medical teams.

To our Colorado providers: Dr. Odekirk, thank you for never giving up on me and for your unending prayers. Dr. Barnes, you have become like family to us and we love you so much. Wes and I can never thank you enough for how you have loved and cared for us both.

To our medical teams in Texas: the entire team and staff at the MD Anderson Cancer Center, my heart is overwhelmed by gratitude for you. I am eternally grateful for you all and pray for you daily.

The support from friends, coworkers, and total strangers who stepped into our lives was unimaginable. We had everything we needed from prayers, donations, fundraisers, letters, gifts, and phone calls. I have never been so inspired in my entire life than by witnessing your loving us the way you did. The love and acts of service were mind-blowing as we felt your care every step of the way. Thank you.

To every person who has been diagnosed with cancer, I carry you with me in my heart. Always remember that you are not alone. You are surrounded by a God who loves you and a community that will never give up on you. My prayer is that this story brings you hope, comfort, joy, and laughter amid your journey. Your life is worth fighting for and you have a great purpose. May God bless you and your caregivers, family, and friends who walk closely with you.

Last but not least, to the one I love the most, I want to thank my Lord and Savior, Jesus Christ. He has given us the amazing gift of eternal life that is freely given to all who receive him as Lord and Savior. I don't have to remain afraid while living because he walks every step of this journey with me. I didn't have to be afraid of dying, because he has a place ready for me in heaven. I will forever serve and love him. My whole purpose in writing this is to share the story that God wrote in my life and so you may know he loves you too. He can become the Lord of your life right now if you ask him to. It will be the best decision you make in your entire life.

Sparkle on!

About the Author

Nicole Body is an author, speaker, and creator of the faith-based cancer blog SparklySurvivor.com. She currently works as the Communications Director for WoodsEdge Community Church. She sings Christmas carols year-round and believes dark chocolate should be its own food group. She doesn't have a shy bone in her body as she shares openly and honestly about her life experiences with vivacious enthusiasm, heartfelt compassion, and Spirit-led encouragement. Her life verse is John 16:33 and is in the heart of everything she writes and speaks about.

She is a complete romantic and is dearly devoted to her husband, Wes. They love ballroom dancing, traveling, and all things Disney with hopes of visiting every Disney park in the world one day. Wes and Nicole are excited to announce that they have a little miracle on the way! They are already completely in love with their little girl, Aurora Elizabeth Body, and can't wait for her to arrive.

Nicole has a true servant's heart demonstrated in her membership in the Junior League, serving at her church, and volunteering at the MD Anderson Cancer Center. When she's not volunteering, she can be found at her local Pure Barre studio, cooking, or spending time with family and friends.

She would love to connect with you at Connect@SparklySurvivor.com or through Instagram, Facebook, or Twitter @SparklySurvivor.

Photo Gallery

Before having their heads shaved

After having their heads shaved

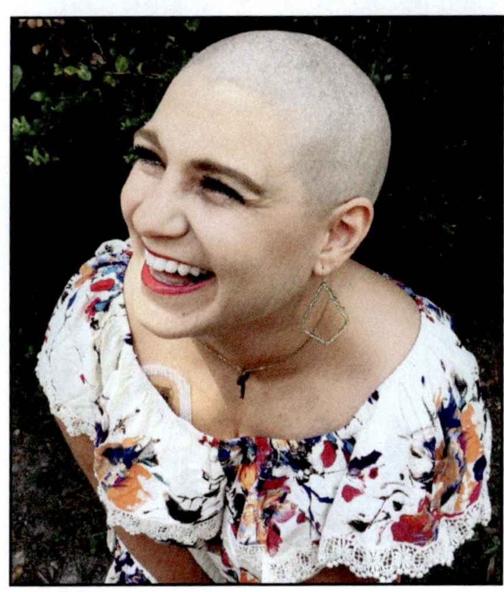

Wes took Nicole out for a photo shoot after her head was shaved.

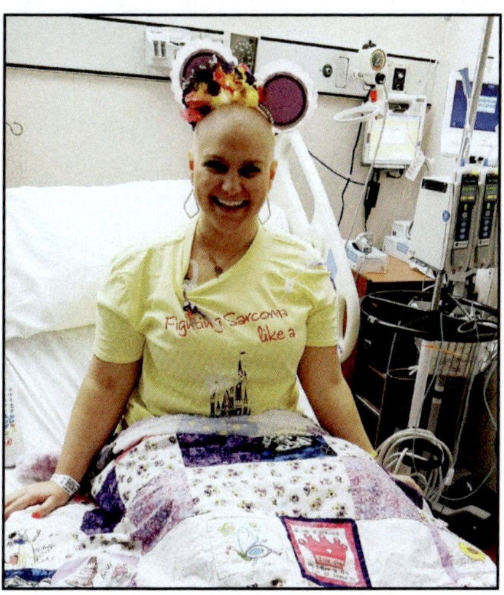

Nicole during a chemotherapy treatment at the MD Anderson Cancer Center.

Photo Gallery

Nicole and Wes out at dinner from Chapter 22, Dating You.

Attending the Christmas Eve service after being discharged from the hospital from surgery early.

Christmas card photo taken during treatment. Photo courtesy of Rick Gentry.

Renewing their vows for their four-year wedding anniversary after Nicole became cancer-free. This took place where they got married: the Della Terra Mountain Chateau in Estes Park, Colorado.

Photo Gallery

Celebrating Nicole's one-year cancer-free anniversary at Walt Disney World in Florida.

Participating in the Race to Cure Sarcoma in Denver.

Wes and Nicole at the United States Capitol in Washington, D.C., at the One Voice Against Cancer Lobby.

Photo Gallery

Volunteering at Children's Hospital Colorado as Kristoff and Anna from Frozen.

Nicole speaking at the Strike Out Sarcoma fundraiser. Photo courtesy of Rey Francisco Photography.